KATE ROBERTS

Kate Roberts

DEREC LLWYD MORGAN

CARDIFF
UNIVERSITY OF WALES PRESS 1991

©University of Wales and the Welsh Arts Council 1991

British Library Cataloguing in Publication Data

Morgan, Derec Llwyd
  Kate Roberts.
  1. Fiction in Welsh. Roberts, Kate, 1891-1985
  I. Title
  891.6632
ISBN 0-7083-1115-6

The publishers wish to thank Plaid Cymru for permission to quote from Kate Roberts's work.

Typeset in Wales by Afal, Cardiff
Designed in Wales by Cloud Nine, Cardiff
Printed in Wales by Gwasg John Penry, Swansea

Preface

This essay was first published in 1974, as a monograph in the *Writers of Wales* series published jointly by the University of Wales Press and the Welsh Arts Council. I have made only very minor changes to the text; but of course it was necessary to add a few paragraphs about the stories Kate Roberts published after 1974. The occasion of its reprinting is the centenary of her birth.

January 1991   *Derec Llwyd Morgan*

I

Art, like the universe, may be infinite, but the individual artist creates a world of his own. In a writer's work this world is an imaginative stock of places and characters and problems, a world to which he gives its own history and perspective, though these sometimes correspond to the history and perspective of our actual time-world. In writing, in creating, the writer can be dedicated to a vision, a theme, a tone, a type of character, or an image, and it is this chosen primary element that forms the axis of his sphere, the axis in its turn regulating the shape of the artist's world, its bias and speed of movement. More often than not, we recognize a storyteller's world by its landscape and its people's behaviour; and when he describes them in later books we notice some repetition, the kind that leads to rediscovery of familiar territory, and, generally, greater understanding of people. This is true of storytelling at all levels, of the thrillers about the 87th precinct no less than of Jane Austen's novels. The more we are told about Ed McBain's New York policemen, it becomes proportionately easier to appreciate the often uneasy sympathy that exists between them. Similarly, repeated visits to West Country drawing-rooms endow us with the familiarity necessary to gauge Jane Austen's contempt of them.

This essay is intended as an introductory description of Kate Roberts's world, what she created, where, and how. Some artistic worlds just grow, but with Kate Roberts it's possible to speak of hers as 'designed', and talk of a design as a blueprint that existed in her imagination before any of her stories were published. From the beginning of her career the force that drove her to write was a 'vision of life'. In a radio interview in 1947 she said:

> When an author gets an idea for a story, it finishes there, until another idea comes. But if you get a vision of life, the second story will thrust itself [upon you] before you finish writing the first.

1

How then is the thirtieth story, say, not a pastiche of the third? Visions are not static, frozen things. When she was asked twenty years later in another interview to explain her unremitting passion for writing, Kate Roberts said:

> In one way my horizons widen because my experience has increased: I have witnessed a great deal of life and have learned from it . . . At the beginning I would see a little bit in front of me, but now my eyes can see the sides as well.

Another of her statements that justifies my reference to a design can be found in *Y Lôn Wen (The White Lane)*, a 'Piece of Autobiography' published in 1960. The book's representative statement is this one:

> Everything important, everything of deep impression, happened to me before 1917.

The greater part of that impression has been printed now as literature.

Kate Roberts's imaginative world is composed of two distinct layers of life. The first, lower layer contains a sad picture of the life of a slate-quarrying community in Arfon, some four miles south of Caernarfon, during the last quarter of the last century and the first quarter of this one. Here are set all her early works — i.e. the books which appeared between 1925 and 1937 — except for three stories which describe working-class life in the coal-mining valleys of Glamorgan during the Great Depression. Obviously, Kate Roberts drew on her own memory and experience for her materials, for she was the daughter of a quarryman and his wife who lived in Rhosgadfan, Caernarfonshire. The background to the stories set in the south was also part of her experience: between 1915 and 1935 she lived (and for most of those years, worked as a teacher) in Glamorgan. From 1935 until her death she lived in Denbigh, and thus knew at first hand the somewhat neurotic contemporary small-town life of north Wales contained in her second layer of literature. All the short stories and novels that deal with this half of her world were published after the Second World War. Some of these later works none the less deal exclusively with the earlier epoch. And only a small few of the characters created to inhabit one of her towns are bereft of the opportunity to burrow and take refuge in the spiritual and emotional security of the older period — that is what links them with the pre-1917 era. Neither is the knowledgeable reader of the later books ever allowed to lose his sense of recognition of that period.

It seems a small world: one character calls Arfon 'an old place like this at the end of the earth, terribly old-fashioned, eating the same thing day after day'. Not that its size matters. Echoing an important point made by Saunders Lewis in the radio interview referred to above, Kate Roberts maintained in a later article that a writer of genius could 'write about his own village for a century, because that village for him represents mankind'. Nor does the fact that it's been constructed from memory and experience make it a poor world. An author transforms his material imaginatively. Indeed, it is this very act of recasting and modifying in appropriate words the temporal and historical raw material around him that makes the author an original creator, and which marks the border between his own world and that of the history books and of *Newsweek* or the *Daily Express*. Yet, as we shall see, Kate Roberts often adopted the historian's style and stance, the preoccupation with periods and dates, movements and specific influences, even in the compass of a simple short story, and so used rhetorical devices which as it were support the heretical view of her work as memoir.

Her world is authentically hers just as Mauriac's Bordeaux is his, or as Georgia is to Carson McCullers, for she was above all things a creator of people, solid, articulate, sensitive people who move and breathe in a land she depicted for their habitation. Her mastery of idiom and syntax was renowned, few of her fellows matched her sensitivity, and the people of her books are so nervously alive that one feels a social historian attempting a description of Edwardian Arfon or mid twentieth-century Denbigh would be inevitably vain if he did not begin his work with an analysis of Kate Roberts's stories, for the characters there and the situations she invented possess the authoritative truth only the genius of imagination can produce. That truth sounds like the deep note of humanity.

II

Perhaps the best way to introduce Kate Roberts to a strange audience, graph her life, and comment upon her imaginative world's connection with the historical world from which she formed it, is to expound upon one of her short stories. I have chosen the story called 'Dychwelyd' *(Returning)* from the collection *Gobaith a Storïau Eraill (Hope and Other Stories)*, published in 1972. I have chosen 'Dychwelyd' firstly because its parts grant us a view of life in Denbigh and Arfon; and secondly because the first two parts are 'realistic' descriptions of the two halves of the world of Kate Roberts, whilst the third part, with the fusing of time present and time past, a masterpiece of sureality, enables us to see what symbolic use she made of these places.

In the short opening part of the story, Kate Roberts describes the mocking of an old woman by a gang of ruffian schoolboys who imitate her manner of barring them from cycling on the private road on which she lives. They then shout at her in 'the dirtiest language she had ever heard'. Later on, the old woman muses:

> In her days school stood for civility. By now it was no better than a home for scamps and its language the language of a country going to the dogs.

The second part of the story portrays the old woman as a young girl (she is named here, Annie) walking the slopes of a mountain to take part in scenes of home. No sooner does she recite a Welsh rhyme commanding a snail to stretch out its horns than they 'jump out like wicket sticks'; Annie and her mother laugh when a kitten stands on a dough-mix; then a rainstorm brings with it care in the shape of fresh underclothes straight from the small oven, and hot broth. The passage throughout is so rich in warm human behaviour, natural description, exact and colourful vocabulary as to convey the

4

harmony that once ordered the earth. Thus it is only natural that Annie should wish to revisit the time and place she remembers so vividly. So, in the third part of 'Dychwelyd', Annie is

> again going towards the mountain. She had decided to do this before going to see her father and mother. It would be so nice to see them again, have a chat by the fire, and tell them about those old swearing ruffian youths.

But it's difficult going, she cannot find the path, her old neighbours don't live where they used to, the quarry is silent, only the distant sea is as it was. Limping along, Annie again comes face to face with a gang of dirty long-haired youngsters, from whose taunts she is rescued by a man who calls her *''y ngenath i' (my girl)* and who escorts her to the village. There she finds her old home:

> There was as it were a veil of mist over the kitchen, her father and mother like shadows in the middle of it. Their faces were of the colour of grey-green putty, their cheeks were hollows and hillocks, their hooked chins and noses nearly touching each other. Yet she could recognize them.

The parents recognize Annie, too. The meal they had prepared for her years ago is now tasteless. Then the mist gradually clears, the faces become more natural; and rather than make her eat her meat and bread and butter, Annie's mother brings from the small oven a dough-cake like the one on which the kitten had stood such a long time back. Afterwards Annie passes two cigarettes to her father and tells him to smoke them in his pipe.

> The mother smiled.
> 'I'll take one, too,' she said, 'I remember how my aunt used to come to our house and smoke a pipe.'
> 'What next?' Annie told herself, in astonishment that was near to fright; she also took one.
> And there they were, the three of them smoking, so happily, so happily. Where were the others? Where were the others? No, she wouldn't ask. Light blue smoke curled up to the sky. The sun disappeared. Dusk descended. Their eyelids began to fall over their eyes as on a statue. The three went to sleep.

The story is a beautiful piece of literature. The richness of the second part contrasts with the social problem of the first as if their juxtaposition was a clash of two cultures, which it is in a way. No one who had been reared in a community as considerate as Annie's could for one moment face the onslaught of the permissive era of her old age unperplexed; and in 'Dychwelyd' the description of childhood is not only an explanation of Annie's defection, it is also a criticism of the ignorance of the present. Neither the lewd-mouthed boys nor their parents could appreciate or identify the plants named and placed so accurately in the second part. (No doubt the man who defends Annie in the third part could do so — but he is probably a native Arfonian.) Notice how Kate Roberts in the final part of the story chooses to refer to objects previously described in the middle part, the dough-mix and the small oven, making them symbols of her people's domestic culture, which again afford a contrast with the supermarket shopping basket of the opening part and the studied kindness of late twentieth-century shop assistants. Notice also how the author restrains Annie from trying to re-create her complete past happiness — she is made not to ask after her brothers and sisters — and is left content in her burrow of memory.

Its style, the sensibility of the prose in 'Dychwelyd', matched by the arranging of symbols, and by the dreamlike vision of its end part, all lift it outside the realm of memoir into the more determinate sphere of fiction.

Yet a budding biographer could easily detect here traces of the real Kate Roberts. Born in 1891, she was, when she wrote 'Dychwelyd', an old woman living alone in Denbigh, as defiant and hardworking as she had been all her life. After graduating in Welsh at the University College of North Wales in 1913, she spent one session at Dolbadarn Elementary School, before moving (after a short period as a supply teacher) in 1915 to Ystalyfera County School in the Swansea Valley, where she taught the poet Gwenallt and Islwyn Williams, the short-story writer. Then she moved to Aberdâr. That was in 1917. In 1928 she married. In 1935 her husband Morris Williams formed a small company and bought Gwasg Gee, the most famous of the Welsh presses and the original home of *Baner ac Amserau Cymru*, to whose pages from then on Kate Roberts contributed hundreds of signed and unsigned articles. After her husband's death in 1946 it was she who kept the business going. Only a nitwit would claim that her other work made her popular in the town (though she reigned a queen in its literary circle). She strived unstintingly to promote the cause of Welsh nationalism in Denbigh and elsewhere in Wales. Her ferocious honesty made her a fearsome figure; but again those who knew her knew her wit and humour and hearty laughter. In retirement, she took her place in the van of those who petitioned and worked for a Welsh-medium primary school in Denbigh, and Ysgol Twm o'r Nant is as much a monument to her spirit as it is a memorial to the eighteenth-century playwright. Like Annie's in 'Dychwelyd', her house was at the end of a private lane. I know that she had often been pestered there by trespassing schoolboys, who seemed to cultivate as a sport the vexing of old disciplinarians, whose principles and belief — Kate Roberts's were at once conservative and revolutionary — no doubt appeared to them totally eccentric.

Of childhood, she had an inexhaustible memory. She shared many reminiscences with Annie. There is a passage in *Y Lôn Wen* where Kate Roberts's mother laughs at the antics of a cat, this time one who sat on her daughter's best Leghorn hat. The autobiography also tells us of the pleasure Kate the child had on the mountain, doing and observing exactly the same things as Annie in the second part of the story. *Y Lôn Wen* is one source of knowledge about the district Annie returns to, a place of quarries and small homesteads, in which hard work was relieved only by neighbourly support and at night-time and in dead of winter by the enjoyment of good company and, sometimes, reading. It is this inheritance of eloquence and literacy which makes Annie despair of the stupidity of her schoolboy baiters. Her father, Kate Roberts tells us, relished both good companionship and reading, 'but he was a slower reader than my mother'. Her mother, extremely capable, inquisitive, quick, forthright, stands out clearly as the great heroine of *Y Lôn Wen*, greater even than the close-knit community of craftsmen itself. And the prevailing strength of her character is undoubtedly what led her daughter to write so much about the roles of motherhood, real and symbolic. Economically, the land of her childhood was a poor place, work in the quarries often broken by stoppages, endangered by sudden death, and the work-force breached by emigration. During the Great War things were much worse, for most of the smaller quarries were closed, and the men who did not enlist in the army had to go away, many to Merseyside, some to the United States, to find work.

Yes, Kate Roberts in old age was a tough old lady. She was not a woman easily crossed. But though Kate Roberts — still like Annie — displayed a bold face, she was thin-skinned, easily hurt, and given to periods of melancholic meditation. Now comes the break with Annie. In the third part of 'Dychwelyd' the heroine does not know the whereabouts of the other members of the family. But her creator was only too conscious of the fate of her brothers and its effect on her. It was four years after the death of her youngest brother, David, in the Great War that she first felt the necessity to write: 'I had to say something or sink'. That was in 1921. In 1947, twenty months after burying Morris Williams, she describes her melancholy in another metaphor: 'I am as if I were moving in a vacuum, looking at life going past'. An unsympathetic reader of Kate Roberts's interviews could be forgiven for thinking she felt she was the only sister who lost a young brother in the blood-bath, and that no other middle-aged wife donned a widow's weeds. But what these tribulations touched was a great sensitive artist; and surely the point is that grief is one of the two main turbines that made up the dynamic of her imagination, the other being a love for a certain way of life on a particular piece of mountain.

Her epic description of this grief and way of life is the novel *Traed Mewn Cyffion* (the Authorized Version, Job xiii 27, has *Feet in the Stocks*, an ugly translation to the Welsh ear, but there is no apt attractive one). It was published in 1936. I call it 'epic' not because it is lengthy — nearly forty years pass in less than two hundred pages — but because, as Emyr Humphreys has noted, it possesses many of the characteristics of the classical epic, heroism, incessant struggle, dangers, a huge time consciousness.

Its heroine is Jane Gruffydd. In 1880 she comes from Llŷn (a place she returns to only once or twice in thirty-five years) to marry Ifan, settles at Ffridd Felen, a smallholding in Foel Arian, and takes part in the battle waged thereabouts against poverty and fate, the Scylla and Charybdis of life here, dangers that are somehow never passed. Burdens are soon loaded upon her, six children in all, tribal jealousy, mortgage repayments, the vagaries of the livestock market, and even though she is abler than most, Owen, her fourth child, early in life associates his mother's sad looks with all adults. The day she had to sell a cow to be slaughtered because it only had three teats on its udder, he remembers asking her

'Mam, what would be if there wasn't anything at all?'
'What do you mean?'
'What would be if there wasn't *anything*, no there [pointing to the sky], absolutely nothing, and we weren't either?'
'It would be very pleasant, my boy,' was her only answer.

Jane Gruffydd's goal was a better life. Llŷn people had come to Arfon before her, hoping that the quarries would sustain them more richly than the land. It was a false hope. She in turn now wants the children to reap benefits that are impossible for Ifan and her. It's the smell of success that keeps her going sometimes. Owen and Twm, the youngest sons, win scholarships to grammar school, but their going to Caernarfon is expensive, and so is the eventual move to the university college at Bangor, but these places promise a better world. After spending a pound on necessities for Owen's journey thence she asks herself

> whether she would be allowed to come to town sometime with the money in her pocket more than her needs. Yes, she would, she would. Owen would come to earn, so would Twm. They would get good salaries; she could then pay her debts and buy a few luxuries.

I have translated *a gâi hi* as 'whether she would be allowed to' (though it may be the subjunctive, 'whether she would') because I feel that Jane Gruffydd is somehow aware of a supernatural oppressive force that perhaps in time will weaken its hold on her: '"There is no reason for things to be so constantly bad; one expects them to improve"'. Wiliam, the third child, is the first in the family to understand what economic social justice really means, and is one of the few in the whole district who realizes what degree of protest and sacrifice is needed to achieve even a semblance of it. Wiliam is at work before we get to know him (as is Elin, the eldest) and it is only in Chapter XI, an interlude, a sort of Homeric summary of things, that he is linked with the Independent Labour Party and trade unionism. Before long, when wages reach rock-bottom, when he can't stand his co-workers' pusillanimity any longer, he moves to south Wales, 'to the ends of the earth'. So, the one crewman ready to defy the jaws of Scylla is taken away.

Injustice exists within the family too. When Ifan's mother dies, her savings are passed on according to her will to Sioned, Ifan and Jane's second daughter, a whipper-snapper of a girl who had served much of her childhood as the medium of her grandmother's irrational dislike of Jane Gruffydd. In youth she serves as a shop assistant in town. From there, through her again, a new trouble oppresses the family. She marries one Bertie Elis who is as gullible and gutless as the acned advertiser of Charles Atlas's body-building course. He was born, I should think, in the birth columns of an English newspaper, a kind of *Daily Mirror* whose reflections of life are exactly his. Had Sioned been a nicer girl, one would say 'Poor Sioned!' but she merits nothing better than her Bertie. We are led to see that her bad luck increases in proportion to her attachment to Bertie's affectations, the chief one being his dull predilection for using English words, stultifying his Welsh. (Bertie soon vanishes from home with his employer's money as swag; and the last time we see Sioned she is in the preliminary stages of purveying her beauty to an army officer in Llandudno.)

Kate Roberts struck this chord, the sound of English meaning estrangement and trouble, in an earlier passage where Jane Gruffydd discusses with the witty and wise Ann Ifans a speech they had just heard at a prize-giving ceremony in Owen's school. Jane speaks first:

'Isn't it a pity one can't understand a bit of English, Ann Ifans?'
'I'm not so sure; one understands quite enough about this old world already. God knows how much pain someone avoids through not knowing English.'

The deepest pain connected with English in *Traed Mewn Cyffion* is the news of Twm's death in the war. It is brought by telegram, which Jane Gruffydd takes to the grocer's for a translation — she believed it was another government form to be filled. The irony of this incident is twofold. One is obvious: the Welsh hear of death in a strange tongue. The second needs clarification. Twm had enlisted only because he was fed up with not being allowed to teach his specialist subject in the school where he worked; that subject was Welsh.

Owen in the novel objects to the war. At the end of the book he sees it as only one of the elements which had hit his parents and community. Like most strugglers they had looked forward to a retirement free of debt and strife, and when that was in sight lo! 'a completely unexpected blow', Twm's death. Owen now sees what Wiliam had seen ten years previously:

It was high time someone stood up to all this injustice. Act. That was the fault in his people. It was in their ability to suffer that they were heroic, not in their ability to do anything against the cause of their suffering.

There is about this final chapter describing Owen's thoughts a certain Telemachian spirit, but Owen hasn't any muscle left to substantiate that spirit's eagerness. Neither has Arfon, nor indeed Europe, for with the closing of *Traed Mewn Cyffion* we are aware of the end of an era. In the course of the novel, Kate Roberts more than once emphasizes how ignorant the Arfonians are of what causes their troubles. But the great paradox of their life after 1918 — and we are now outside the borders of *Traed Mewn Cyffion* — was that education and army experience and emigration not only gave their children a wider view of the globe, it also made their land susceptible to all sorts of foreign influences which by the third part of 'Dychwelyd' have all but destroyed its native culture. Isolation had been their fortress, as it was for the people of the Arofan tribe in Thomas Gwynn Jones's 'Argoed', or, in another context, for Carson McCullers's simple folk in *The Ballad of the Sad Café*. These seduced and displaced Arfonians can be identified later on with many of the anxious characters of Kate Roberts's post-1949 books, grown-ups bereft of their parents' wise parochialism, stoicism and cultural security.

Walter Bagehot once said of Dickens: 'He describes London like a special correspondent for posterity'. Strange as it may seem, for unlike Dickens's novels it is not chock-a-block of detailed descriptions, *Traed Mewn Cyffion* too has this quality of history. Yet so much acreage is left undescribed, so many emotions are left unravelled, so many relationships left unparticularized! Why? It is not because Kate Roberts has neglected detail, no, the novel more than adequately deals with its chosen subjects. Rather, after reading it many times, one is left with the impression that she created it so as to reflect the poverty of the land — T. H. Parry-Williams's *moelni maith (vast sparseness)* — and the life lived there. In other artistic terms, her oils are like Kyffin Williams's, lighting, touching up *telling* details.

III

Kate Roberts used some of the acres and emotions and relationships unfilled and unfulfilled in *Traed Mewn Cyffion* in later books. Some she had dwelled upon previously. She returns to treat at length of the subject of the final third of *Traed Mewn Cyffion* in the novel *Tegwch y Bore (Fair Weather in the Morning, 1967), which was first printed in weekly instalments in *Baner ac Amserau Cymru* during 1957 and 1958. Kate Roberts then put it away, 'thinking it was not good enough to be published'. This is not a note of false modesty; nor is it a lock-out judgement. True enough, *Tegwch y Bore* is not as synoptic as *Traed Mewn Cyffion*, nor does it possess the tremendous poetic force of the earlier novel, it is more prosaic, the main figure of speech here is the short simile not the bald symbol, in parts it is repetitive. But there is no denying its efficacy as saga. I wonder how near the truth I am when I suggest that one of the chief reasons why Kate Roberts was reluctant to issue it in book-form was that its story — so, so close to her own, it is almost autobiography in parts — had been carved off the bone and it hurt.

Tegwch y Bore deals with the years between 1913 and 1917 from the point of view of Ann Owen, a young responsible graduate who, because of her femininity more than anything else, is left during the Great War to guard and sometimes muster her family while her younger brother Bobi goes to fight and dies, and while her boy-friend Richard joins the medical corps, is wounded, but not fatally. She is in part like Owen, she rebels against her schoolmaster as did Twm; and Bobi's going to war is a carbon copy of Twm's going. But the emphases in the two novels are different. In *Tegwch y Bore* home is a place to return to or to hear from, it is not the axle of affairs as it was in *Traed Mewn Cyffion*, and this more than anything actually said in the course of the novel is its mark of change. Home is never the same for people gone away — Ann teaching at Ynys y Grug, south Wales (which is Ystalyfera fictionalized), Bobi at war, brother Huw working in Liverpool, their father considering the move also. Thus, the life of Arfon, or what remains of it, is described only periodically — the reader should *know* it from previous books by Kate Roberts. Movement and exile have replaced stability and security. But such diversion affords the author the opportunity to describe the life of the period in other parts of Wales and in London. Ann visits Richard's home in Anglesey, she describes the narrow unthinking chapel-limited morality of the time as it is concentrated in Mrs Ifans, her landlady at Blaen Ddôl, whence she moved to Ynys y Grug, a kinder society by half. A large number of minor characters populate these places, all of whom are introduced in relation to Ann, her love, indignation, anxiety and hope being the life-forces of this saga of war. As *Traed Mewn Cyffion* is fathomless and still, *Tegwch y Bore* is panoramic and spasmodic; the first was poetic, in the later novel there are discussions on theological and ethical topics, numerous descriptions of clothes and furniture, things akin to the speculative nature of what I feign to call the prosaic novel (but I do not use the adjective derogatively).

Occasionally we do see the pattern of events and hopes that did not prepare Owen and his family for the débâcle of 1914, and that unfailingly reminds us of the earlier novel, whose depth, so to speak, receives the explosive charge of this one. Take as an example these sentences of Ann's musing on the progress of life and the meaning of this war:

> Things had been worse in her grandparents' time, and worse still in their parents' time, and it appeared that things were on the verge of being better for her parents when the war came. War was so new, so strange to the world of turning the poor crust of land on the smallholding, to splitting seamed rocks in the quarry. They knew in time past about striving, striving for a place for their holdings on the common, with the landlord, but they knew then what they were fighting for, and there was no life lost. But now they did not know what they were fighting for. They were blind people groping for the partitions of the world. If anything happened to their children, they could never afterwards delight in a better world if there should come a better world.

The first part of this passage echoes a talk between Jane Gruffydd and Ann Ifans in *Traed Mewn Cyffion* and echoes also the unspoken

13

contention of the first half of that novel where the old Sioned Gruffydd, Jane's mother-in-law, represents an old generation that came from Llŷn's hardship to suffer Arfon's. '. . . they did not know what they were fighting for', Ann Owen muses. Earlier she had found herself doubting all pronouncements about the war, certain only that she was

> a Welshwoman, and that this was not Wales's war. She wasn't so sure what would become of Wales should England lose the war, but she came to hate hearing people talk about 'dying for their country'.

This was undoubtedly Kate Roberts's own opinion of it. But compare with this a piece of narrative from *Traed Mewn Cyffion*. It is 1917:

> By now [the people of Foel Arian] did not believe at all that the war's purpose was to defend the rights of small nations, and that it was a war to end wars, nor did they believe one country was to blame more than another, but they had come to believe that there were people in every country who liked war, and that they used their sons to their own advantage. These were the aristocracy, the same people who oppressed them in the quarry, and sucked their blood and turned it into gold for themselves.

These passages constitute some of the most poignant social criticism made in Welsh literature in the twentieth century, and can be placed side by side with Gwenallt's indignant ferocity in poetry. Couple with the last sentence (about 'delight in a better world') quoted above from *Tegwch y Bore*, Owen's thoughts, and note the symbolism of the clothes:

> He remembered hearing Ann Ifans saying sometime how grand his mother's clothes were when she first came to the district. She never got new clothes now. She had some after Twm's death, but she had never worn them after that.

All reason for joy is past. The world changeth!

Like mother, like daughter (for Ann Owen can be called Jane Gruffydd's daughter). When the news came of Bobi's death, she is dejected as Jane Gruffydd was at the news of Twm's. And no wonder. Throughout Part I of *Tegwch y Bore* Ann is a mother-figure to Bobi. At his first communion, she pities him and his fellows because they are now turning their backs on innocence, and in that pity 'she felt Bobi's fine hair on her face when he was a baby in a shawl in her arm', the hair 'like an unopened buttercup fitting like a cap on his head'. For him she was already adult and adoring. It is to her lodgings that Bobi comes when he's fed-up or famished, and as far as we know it is she who worries most when he goes to the army.

Yet, another young man — a stiffer, nobler, but still somewhat dependent young man — bids for her favours, Richard Edmwnd, BA. And it is a competition. Richard Edmwnd is an orphan, drawn towards Ann by the responsible elements in her character. Thus she is a mother-figure for him as well. '"I have no home, . . . nor father nor mother nor brother nor sister, I lost my parents when I was young."' Ann in her bed one night early in the book has to repress her passionate thoughts about him; but Richard only very gradually gains our respect as a possible lover of female flesh; for so long he is such a flannel, and so over-cautious. Granted, his advancement in *amour* is hindered by two things. The first is a code of manners — the young people of Gwynedd in 1914 did not make love as openly as some magazines lead us to believe the students of today make love: Lloyd George's influence did not spread that far home! Secondly, it's only fair to note that Kate Roberts was ill at ease on the subject of love, especially carnal love. So until the last few chapters Richard Edmwnd must remain the epitome of tedious solicitude.

Love, in Kate Roberts's work, is nearly always polluted. Wiliam in *Traed Mewn Cyffion* obviously enjoys a fruitful married life with his south Walian bride, but we did not witness the courting or the nuptials there. Sometimes love is unilateral, sometimes mixed with guilt or jealousy. *Tegwch y Bore* reaches its pitch when Ann, after losing Bobi, chooses selfishly to solace herself with his memory, her favourite child, rather than accept the comfort of Richard's love. For some time, she could not tell Richard

how jealous she was that he was still alive. Perhaps this jealousy would disappear if he kept away. But what would take its place? Would any feeling come back except bad feeling?

Home offers the only comfort: '"there we are all like eyes on the same string"'. But in the penultimate chapter of the novel a new feeling wells in her

> like the current of a soft stream . . . She wanted to see [Richard] more than anything in the world. It was a miracle, this sudden feeling that came over her. She could not explain it. It was there, that's all.

Although this is a romantic ending, it is not the ending of conventional romance. Richard and Ann scarcely make a pair of *Woman's Own* teachers cooing at each other over staffroom teacups, nor are they Isaac and Rebecca intent upon forging a love relationship for the greater glory of God. No, the resurgence of life in Ann Owen is to be identified with the reformation of other characters Kate Roberts wrote about in the fifties and sixties, identified with similarly sudden gusts of recovery, all of them experienced by women whose mainspring, their reason for living and striving, had been broken. Ann grasps Richard as another character, say Lora Ffennig, grasps the remnants of family life.

So, this novel about Ann the mother-figure ends on a note totally different from that on which the great mother Jane Gruffydd's *Traed Mewn Cyffion* ends. The end there is spectral: Owen, mother's wise son, sees his dead brother's initials carved on a mountain stone; the end of *Tegwch y Bore* is forward-looking, spirited. These two aspects form a contrast that is one of the most important dualities in Kate Roberts's work, a duality that we must recognize — as does Dafydd Glyn Jones — as 'one of the great paradoxes that give vitality and depth' to her literature; though, to be truthful, I sometimes find the suddenness of the transformation a bit hard to accept.

Backward- and forward-looking, what the author sees at the end of both novels is Time. A metaphysicist would not be way off the mark if he chose to see *Traed Mewn Cyffion* as an appeal to Time, and the end of *Tegwch y Bore* as an indication of Ann Owen's acceptance of Time's illogical judgement. The first novel, never hurried, begins on a hot Sunday afternoon in June 1880. Births and deaths are carefully, annalistically recorded: e.g. 'A few months after Ifan resumed working, their third child was born and he was called Wiliam, and two years hence another son was born to them and he was called Owen'. Age disperses the family, the fixed holiday of Christmas marks their annual reunion. Such slow sure ordering makes manifest Jane

Gruffydd's faith in the eventual coming of a better life, as if the edge of each and every page in the book could be the horizon of a new dawn, and Time the cloud-carriage of her messiah. Time is not so hallowed in *Tegwch y Bore*. Its acts are more multifarious, happenings proliferate, so that Kate Roberts here is able to mark Time by meals, meetings, meals above all, a good meal reflecting or exciting good feeling, a poor meal presaging bad times, thus identifying temper with *tempus*. Very very often in the later books the characters, who are sceptical of the Age of Progress's belief in Time-as-messiah, find themselves looking to a good meal or a pretty tea-party for consolation, making of eating not a Time marker but rather its rebutter. The other mark of Time in Kate Roberts's works is the registering of dress fashions. Stays and stomachs certainly give solidity to an author's creation, and make psychology and history visible.

IV

In my comments on *Traed Mewn Cyffion* I talked of unparticularized relationships. One I had in mind was the relationship between the children as children. Kate Roberts had a rare gift for writing well and wittily about children, and, I suppose, one reason why she did not paint too detailed a picture of them here was that she had already, nine years previously, traced that part of her world in *Deian a Loli* (*Deian and Loli*, twins), 1927, and again in 1930 in *Laura Jones* (Loli now eleven years old). Perhaps some will find this a strange notion, but Kate Roberts knew full well how the parts of her creation were interconnected. In the opening paragraph of the chapter on 'Other Types of Culture' in *Y Lôn Wen* she states: 'I have described our literary festival in *Traed Mewn Cyffion*, therefore its history here will be short, though it was an important part of a district's culture'. It would not have surprised me had there been a footnote in the novel to explain that Elin, Wiliam, and, later, Bet's childhood pass unnoticed because childhood had been described in *Deian a Loli*.

In 1959 Kate Roberts added another volume to her literature of childhood, a collection of stories called *Te yn y Grug* (*Tea in the Heather*). All three books are situated in the author's home district, on the slopes of what she calls Moel y Grug and Mynydd y Grug, the same mountain (again) that Annie returned to in 'Dychwelyd'. The period described is the turn of the century: Russia and Japan were at war when Deian and Loli sat their scholarship examinations, so they were ten or eleven in 1905.*

---

*There is an anachronism in *Laura Jones*. During Loli's first term in service, the winter of 1905-06, she goes to see a performance of *Beddau'r Proffwydi*. I assume this was W.J. Gruffydd's well-known play. It was first published in 1913.

Let's look, to begin with, at *Deian a Loli* and *Laura Jones*. From one point of view *Deian a Loli* makes strange reading, for there is in it a tension created by the pull, in one direction, of the freedom given to the children to roam, flee from home, play truant — freedom that convincingly cuts them off from the responsibility of adult life — and, from the other direction, the pull of the author's ostensible interference, which effectively anchors the children's lives to their parents' plight. Loli's difficulties in arithmetic are compared to her mother Elin Jôs's, 'who never had many opportunities to add anything up, save her troubles'. This comparison is reworded later on when the author notes: 'Some children's lives are made up of toil and trouble exactly like a grown-up's life'. But Kate Roberts's interventions, far from serving to dispirit us by emphasizing the sober truth about life on Moel y Grug, rather render it for the time being more enjoyable, jolly, yes, childlike, for the naïvety of some of her comparisons and her simple explanations make us, her readers, feel like children. After reading about the struggle of three generations in the epic *Traed Mewn Cyffion*, open *Deian a Loli* and what do you get? — a lyrical paragraph on the very same struggle, but much smaller and sweet:

Deian and Loli were twins, living in a smallholding called Bwlch y Gwynt, on the slopes of Moel y Grug. A smallholding is a little farm, and the father of the children who live there must go to the quarry, or some other place, to earn money. When Deian and Loli's grandfather was a little boy there wasn't one Bwlch y Gwynt on the mountain. It was wild moorland, and the old man walked past it in his two big clogs every Monday morning and every Saturday afternoon, on the way to Llanberis Quarry and back. By starting out to work about four on a Monday morning, by working hard all week, and sleeping in the barracks, Elis Jôs earned pennies enough to go to the town one Saturday afternoon to buy the land from the Government. Then he built the house, enclosed the land, and by the time he died Bwlch y Gwynt was as good a smallholding as any in the district.

Through the children we get to know Kate Roberts's other creatures, the animals of the smallholding, some of whom became for her in later years subjects of fantasy, but who are now economic realities, friends also, and once when a monkey comes to Moel y Grug a source of fascination.

But Time catches up with Deian and Loli too. We realize very early on that the boy's application will take him to grammar school, while Loli, only a few years after playing doll's house, must go into domestic service. The end of *Deian a Loli*, like that of *Traed Mewn Cyffion*'s, notes a dispersion and loss. That Deian is the only one from his school who obtains a scholarship merely shows how wide the gap between him and Loli could eventually be. Anyway, Deian becomes David Jones, Loli Laura Jones.

Laura Jones is not an exciting sequel. It is made up of letters to and by and about Laura in her new employment, and describes aspects of the socio-cultural life of a Welsh village in the first decade of this century. I dare say that had it been written by someone other than Kate Roberts it would have been forgotten long ago. The author's intrusions here are more awkward, the characterization more sketchy, the occasional comic scene stereotyped, the outcome melodramatic (though, to be fair, the ending again is one of natural divergence). We read the book because it is part and parcel of Kate Roberts's world, and though, like Greenland, it adds little in the way of fortune or fable to the world, the globe would seem much barer without it. *Laura Jones* can be viewed as the *reductio ad absurdum* of the principles of Kate Roberts's fiction. In most of her early books little happens; in *Laura Jones*, if one discounts Loli's departure from Bwlch y Gwynt at the very beginning, the staging of a play is just about the only event here. Loli's confinement to the farm where she serves — everybody's, come to that — accentuates the microcosmic features of Kate Roberts's geography. And repetition of fact, such as one would expect in letters, symbolizes her early (but not lasting) rejection of novelty. One thing (more a thought than an event, though that too) that ruffles the pages here is Loli's asking the greatest of all questions about Life, worded with absurd economy. But it is a question that is asked time and again in Kate Roberts's books:

> Some strange ideas came into Loli's head while she was looking at [the pigs]. The pigs eating and procreating only to be food for people. People eating — and for what? She working and getting tired in Garreg Lwyd — and for what? Nain having finished working and finished getting tired — and for what?

Laura Jones does support life, and one or two of its characters, especially Andreas, are affectionate, unforgettable. Furthermore, it adds a new dimension to our knowledge of Loli's, and the author's, attitude towards education and literature.

Those who have read Chapter V of *Y Lôn Wen* will know that the school Deian and Loli attended was a near replica of Kate Roberts's school at Rhostryfan (there was no school then in Rhosgadfan). The twins' behaviour is much a reflection of her's. Sums were the staple diet at Rhostryfan, the very bane of Loli's life. Now she was a bright sensitive girl, with a gift for imagining things way beyond the ken of her schoolmaster. For her the Roman remains on the outskirts of Segontium were not a pattern of semi-submerged stones but, by moonlight, an apparition of soldiers. Asked in class to describe a cat, Loli *became* a cat. Deian on the other hand could only see a cat as a furry animal with two ears, two eyes, and four legs, and he could have been describing a leopard for all he felt or said; but Deian for that got a 'Very Good'. In the scholarship examination he merely rewrote a prepared essay on the Russio-Japanese War memorized the night before, whilst Loli wrote about her lunchtime experiences in Caernarfon castle. Deian passed, she didn't. But of course his sums were right. The gist of Kate Roberts's criticism of contemporary education was that it did not encourage anyone to be imaginative, did not foster 'character', tended to make children wary and unoriginal, teachers impatient, punishing. (By the way, Olwen Samuel in an excellent essay in *Kate Roberts: Cyfrol Deyrnged* writes that Kate Roberts herself was a first-class, inspired teacher who never felt bound by her curriculum.)

But even if Loli had passed her exam, it is doubtful whether she could have taken up her scholarship. The family could not afford to send two to Caernarfon; moreover, Elin Jôs saw no reason for sending a girl to county school.

> 'Girls will only marry,' she said (as if boys didn't).
> 'No matter,' said her husband, 'she'll have the education, no-one can go to her head to steal that.'

This is an echo of another piece noting the same opinions published by the author in the twenties; it was to be echoed again in 1932, in *Ffarwel i Addysg (Goodbye to Education)*, a comedy in three acts. Gwen is the heroine of the play, well supported as women's liberator by her Aunt Sara (the antithesis of Elin Jôs) who sternly maintains that 'the world is not held together by Central Grade Schools.'

and again,

'A little bit of education wouldn't harm anybody if he did nothing but feed pigs!'

For her part, Gwen reckons that had her grandfather been able to send her father to college, he would understand education to be something valuable for its own sake.

Kate Roberts here of course, ever so uncontroversially from our standpoint, but in 1932 dashingly enough, is flying in the face of the Welsh who employed her and read her books, the rising professional Welsh among them, those who had made a god of education and called him by his initials, BA. They could not (or would not) see that the god had a foreign face, only that he demanded sacrifices and would thus surely reward the Abrahams. Eternity in his ether was measured in timetables, his grace was duty-bound. As for his priests, both Ann Owen and Twm Gruffydd would agree with Gwen that they are '"trained to spin out money"' and that they '"tire and age before their time in attempting to stuff things into the heads of dull children"'. Grammar school would have spoiled Loli. A redeeming feature of *Laura Jones* is that the girl in the episode describing the play is seen to learn more about the nature of literature than she could ever learn in official lessons; by then she already knew of the inspiratory powers of books. Poor Deian! The system created by the 1870 commandment served, second only to the 1914-18 War, to sever the young men and women of his country from their roots by Anglicizing them in tongue and attitude, and by teaching them nothing that would enhance their pride in the Welsh inheritance. The advantage of education, Kate Roberts makes us realize, was escape, was exile, dissociation, certified cultural suicide.

Sent down from college, Gwen in *Ffarwel i Addysg* is rightly impenitent. She was sent down after being caught in her boyfriend's lodgings. Her defence is that she was following her instinct, her libido. Sex as such — as I have already intimated — is rarely described in Kate Roberts's books, a reticence that reflects her upbringing more than a personal disinclination or phobia. It is the one life-force missing from her books. Some would have been better for its

22

inclusion. I think especially of Y Byw sy'n Cysgu (It is the Living who Sleep, 1956), where a review of Lora Ffennig's sexual relationship with her husband would have cast considerable light on one or two problems. There were signs early on in her literary career, as the first act of Ffarwel i Addysg shows, that Kate Roberts could have countered D. H. Lawrence's novels of masculine oppression with a work or two advancing the theories of modern feminism. Another of these signs is Ysgolfeistr y Bwlch (The Schoolmaster at Bwlch). Two chapters of this unfinished novel were published in Y Llenor in 1926 and 1927. They concern Jennat Thomas, an unqualified teacher nearing what Jean Brodie later called her 'prime' but what Kate Roberts calls 'twenty-eight years of age, a great age to be unmarried in 1896'. Jennat's senses had been aroused before, therefore she understands her craving. Having fancied the schoolmaster she decides to seek him out:

> Jennat was not one of those meek people who believed that love fell like a bolt from the blue. She believed that everybody could get married if he put his mind to it, and she was going to act according to her belief.

She does corner her man, but Chapter II is little more than a dialogue in which she's severely critical of her profession. It ends with the schoolmaster proposing to take her for a walk round the quay. Chapter III could have been a revelation! Is Ysgolfeistr y Bwlch a piece written in reaction to the subjugation of women and the repressions this caused, or is it an isolated story about a sensual woman who has had more than enough of classwork? I think it is a work of criticism, because Jennat takes her place easily in that team composed of Gwen and Ann Owen. In a more affluent and permissive era the three of them would have joined ranks with the feminist fighters.

Not one of them possesses Winni Ffinni Hadog's lack of inhibition. Winni is the star of Te yn y Grug, of all Kate Roberts's girls the one, significantly, who knows most about the seamier side of sex and rough married life. This book is a collection of eight brilliantly penetrative stories which portray the life of three girls in Arfon, again at the turn of the century, Winni, an outcast, the unkempt stepdaughter of a slattern called Lisi Jên, Mair the minister's daughter, prim, baptized in starch, and Begw, of the three the 'normal' girl around whose life the stories turn. Begw's normality is established in the first three stories,

stories of sickness, Mair's snobbishness, and of social habits — it is established, that is, before Winni makes her appearance as if from another world: '"Is it true that you're a witch?"' said Begw. In time Begw senses that Winni's tough ways and speech mark a character that is basically composed of some of the very best human passions and attributes, love (she cares greatly for her stepbrother), candour (in dealing with Mair), and a sense of justice. But could she be asked to tea? Would Begw's mother, Elin Gruffydd, see these qualities in Winni? The vixen had railed against her father, openly hated Lisi Jên, was an excellent swearer; defiant, she had plans for an escape to London to serve Queen Victoria. Could this human tree of knowledge step into *their* garden, next door to the minister? Elin Gruffydd readily consents. But that tea marks a turning-point in Winni's life. Elin Gruffydd, as forthright as Winni and respectable to boot, seeks to reform the adult child and in the ends succeeds. What we have at the end of *Te yn y Grug* is the subjugation of a rebel mountain-girl sent down to Caernarfon to serve an emporium empress. The feminine demon is controlled, the mystery of vitality ruled, measured, and Kate Roberts has reiterated one of her important tenets, 'that nothing in this world exists except change'.

See here in Kate Roberts's matriarchal society how a woman like Elin Gruffydd, not given at all to the niceties usually associated with the fair sex, disciplines this girl, destroys her libido not for any civil reason but because the conditions of economic life in Arfon make discipline necessary. Winni's tragedy is not her home, it is her homeland, it is Mother Earth that makes her in her new clean state resemble, as Elin Gruffydd observes, her late natural mother. This compulsion to compromise with the harshness of the environment is all the more forceful in *Te yn y Grug* because it is such a happy book, and could have ended on a much happier note still. But had she allowed this favourite to fly, Kate Roberts would simply not be Kate Roberts.

V

Deian a Loli is a novel, each chapter portraying an episode of life. *Te yn y Grug* is described as a volume of short stories, and although they do possess a structural independence Begw's presence in them all gives the book the kind of unity associated with the novel. This dichotomy is a feature of several of Kate Roberts's books. One she calls 'a long short story', another 'a short long story'. When she began to write, the short story was not a very popular form in Welsh. By the end of her career she had written more short stories than any other author in the language; and she began her career as a short-story writer. By the early twenties, R. Hughes Williams, R. Dewi Williams, and later E. Tegla Davies, Moelona, J. J. Williams and R. G. Berry had published a few. R. Hughes Williams's example could have been a spur to her, for he was a native of Rhostryfan. But she was without doubt the first great practitioner of the form in Welsh. In 1931 Kate Roberts published a survey of the Welsh short story which shows how thoroughly she had studied its technique, the width of her reading, and how she had avoided the weaknesses of the stories written by the two Williamses. R. Dewi Williams's style, in her opinion, was too turgid: he strained too much after extraordinary similes, made many that were unnecessary, and took most of them from the Bible:

> It could be said that Mr Dewi Williams worries more about his similes than his story, and consequently [the] author becomes unfaithful to himself, and one feels he is not sincere.

R. Hughes Williams is different:

> The first thing we feel about him is that he is sincere. There's no nonsense about his style. He says what he has to say in a short direct manner. In truth we feel that he has something to say about life and has no time to worry about frills.

He too had his faults: he kept too close to the realities of life, failed to 'create' imaginative life, and was prone to write stories in which something had to happen. That happening for him was always a death. The fashionable story in 1931 was the story 'in which nothing much happened and which had no development of a character'. Kate Roberts significantly adds:

> it's one thing to write [such a story] but quite another thing to invest it all with a deep mystical meaning as Chekov and Katherine Mansfield could do.

Her main reason for adopting the short story was that it accommodated her kind of imagination well: 'one thing crossing the mind, seeing in that thing material for a story, and thinking perhaps there wasn't time to produce a novel, [even] if the idea came.' Over and over again in the twenties she rued about having no time to write a lengthy work: that is why she did not carry on with *Ysgolfeistr y Bwlch*, or so she said. She argued too, in an article on 'The Welsh Novel' in 1928, that good prose literature could be produced only where the Welsh language was still strong. She feared that the prose renaissance had come too late, for a monoglot Welsh society — for Kate Roberts the necessary soil for a Welsh novel — was a thing destroyed for ever, life in contemporary Wales being, she maintained, paltry, Anglicized, 'a field unworthy of a novelist's dedication'.

Sixty years later such an idea seems quite unreasonable. Several pretty good novelists have managed to till that 'unworthy' field not unsuccessfully — and have done so, in part, by following the lead given by an older Kate Roberts. It is true that what the younger writers have written are not novels in classical Welsh, it is not the Welsh of a Jeremi Owen or an Ifan Gruffydd, richly idiomatic, accomplished, familiar, but their idiom and style (as they should be) are suited to their subjects. And of course some novelists do spin out idiomatic Welsh, for a dedicated author deprived of monolingualism can learn much by studying his language as it has been used by classical authors through the ages.

When Kate Roberts wrote about the prose renaissance coming too late I believe she confused the issue. That awakening had happened. The fulsome and rich pages of the magazine *Y Llenor* (in which her essay was published) testify to it. W. J. Gruffydd, Kate Roberts herself,

T. H. Parry-Williams, R. T. Jenkins, G. J. Williams, D. J. Williams and Saunders Lewis all contributed to it, all of them, except for Saunders Lewis, brought up in Welsh communities that had survived long enough to nurture *them* and make them all antagonists of the anaemic educators who sought to make Welsh literature utilitarian. In that same essay, Kate Roberts adamantly refuses to toe the line of literature as a medium that could attract 'adults and children to take an interest in the Welsh language'.

VI

Her first collection of stories was published in 1925. It was called *O Gors y Bryniau (From the Marsh of the Hills)*. It is the testament of an artist following her own vision, caring nothing for the political and quasi-educational problems touched upon in my previous paragraphs — problems that will, I'm afraid, form the periphery of Welsh literary life as long as the language is in peril. Some of the stories in *O Gors y Bryniau* are so vibrant with personality and pain, they are as memorable as powerful short poems. Later the author tended to regard their ideals as 'foreign ideals', but we can see here the beginnings of several imaginative patterns that came to form the shape of her world.

The book's most famous story is 'Henaint' *(Old Age)*. Freudians and latter-day feminists would wage a battle royal for the pleasure of possessing the sole right to interpret this one. Very little happens here; we remember 'Henaint' for its chief character and its eerie significance. The narrator is Wil, who acts as intermediary between an old childhood friend, Twm, who is hopelessly ill, and Twm's mother. She is moonstruck, and her memory is fading fast. Four times Wil goes there, each time her memory is worse: she can remember the merriment of her courting days but not her son. The fourth time it is one o'clock in the afternoon, the old woman is on her doorstep, out 'to look around before dusk falls'. Wil tells her:

> 'It's some bad news I've got for you, old woman. Twm, poor chap, has left us.'
>   'Twm,' she said, 'what Twm?'
> 'But Twm your son, your youngest son,' I said.
> She stared vacantly, and said:
>   'I don't know him, y'see.'

The old woman's statement shocks Wil more than Twm's death. It contains not merely the finality of death but somehow captures the very void of meaning; and the myth powerfully made manifest is that of the Woman-Mother as 'the chaos whence all have come and whither all must one day return'. Twm had died in his mother's mind before he died in Nature, and the old woman seems to be Nothingness personified, Loli's question *for what?* given flesh. Although Kate Roberts's world is hard sometimes sympathy is not hard to find for the society is kind, but here Wil has heard the earth speak, and there is no consolation.

But then, when Kate Roberts speaks of some of the stories in *O Gors y Bryniau* as 'foreign' to her, perhaps she is referring to the consolations that seal their endings. In one a widow finds consolation in feeding a calf; in another a wife receives a picture-post letter from her exiled husband; in a third a mother has the opportunity to pay off an old score with her son's former employer. These women, in later books, would have been left to suffer — that suffering being a kind of affinity between them and the land on which they linger and live. Later still, of course, the hope or happiness described here as consolation was to become a commonplace at the end of Kate Roberts's novels and stories. So what was in her view a foreign trait in her earlier literature about a poor but close-knit community became, in her later literature describing the more dispersed, lonely society of the post-war period, a predictable familiar characteristic.

Some of these stories are not what we came to expect of her books, nevertheless most of them contain pains, ideas or images which became permanent parts of her world. They are her imaginative habits. Their roots are grounded in Kate Roberts's own experience, and in the experience of the Arfonians among whom she was reared. For instance: people who had grown used to hard work in the quarries and on smallholdings — in a woman's case, in the home and in outhouses — found it difficult to retire. Such a pair were Wiliam and Margiad Gruffydd in 'Newid Byd' (*A Change of World*), who make the accustomed shift from their smallholding to what is called in Arfon a *tŷ moel*, an ordinary private house with no land attached to it, only a garden. Wiliam Gruffydd cannot easily limit himself to the garden after so many years on fields — Kate Roberts herself confesses in an early essay to having a 'feeling' for fields — and cannot live happily alone after the comradeship of the quarry's cabin. 'Yes, Wiliam

Gruffydd had a longing for the quarry'. But going back is a disaster: it is walking in the face of Time Past. When he gets there he finds his old authority superseded, his place in the cabin occupied, indeed his death foreshadowed.

Another fixture in the fiction is the kind quiet father (Wiliam Gruffydd himself is one), the father who contributes the still sympathy usually found, in patriarchal societies, in the mother. In Arfon the emotional roles are reversed. Seldom is the father forceful. Even Twm Ffinni Hadog, drunk and bad tempered, comes to heel when Lisi Jên calls or when Elin Gruffydd puts him in his place. The chapter on 'My Father' in *Y Lôn Wen* describes them all. Her brother David in part suggested Twm in *Traed Mewn Cyffion* and Bobi in *Tegwch y Bore*. The autobiography does not mention the young members of the family, but Bobi's ill-fated apprenticeship is a repetition of an earlier apprenticeship abandoned for the same reason by Huw in *O Gors y Bryniau*, and the similarity suggests a known historical precedent, perhaps something that happened to David during the early years of the Great War.

I will mention two other recurrences here. There is the community's sense of time, a sense as innate as an animal's. Although I write of it as something belonging to Kate Roberts's community, I dare say it characterizes every society not bound by mechanical clock or calendar: it is a primitive sense, an instinct. In the story 'Yr Athronydd' *(The Philosopher)* in the 1925 collection, we are told in one place that Ifan had no idea what time of year it was:

> but he remembered that the children were playing 'London', and that happened always in spring. That's how his mother used to name the year's seasons. The seasons for her were top-spinning time, skipping time.

These sentences link with a passage in *Y Lôn Wen* where Kate Roberts says that one thing she could never understand was —

> How do children know when to change from one game to another? Children do not play all kinds of games indiscriminately, but there will come a hot fever of playing hoop, of playing marbles, playing top, or playing kite. No-one knows the hour or day the fever starts, but it starts in every district at once. The children of Pwllheli and the children of Caernarfon, the children of Waunfawr and the children of Felinheli play

the same thing at the same time of the year. For me this is one of Creation's mysteries.

As far as I can judge, affluence, the coming of manufactured toys and the migration of people from their tribal bases have made this mystery a mystery of the past — the recent past, it is true, for I was aware of it on the borders of Glamorgan and Carmarthenshire as late as the mid fifties. But let us return to consider its effect on fiction. Where such notes on Time occur they serve to remove the stories into a haze of ultra-sensitivity not far below the magical stratosphere where the figures of the Fourth Branch of the Mabinogi live.

I suppose readers forty years ago would not have found these ideas about Time so strange, but readers change, and that's why each generation should build its own criticism of an author. In Kate Roberts's books, children are not the only ones who read Time's secret signs. They are but inheritors of this 'ability'. Indeed, it takes on a more sinister aspect in their elders: on certain days of the year, they *go* somewhere, are drawn Hamelin-like in a horde, so strangely that one thinks of the Robertsian Arfon as a mountainside abandoned every Whit Monday and Ascension Thursday when the men's clubs march through Caernarfon, abandoned because a deep call has been answered. In the title-story of the collection *Rhigolau Bywyd a Storïau Eraill (Life's Beaten Tracks and Other Stories)* published in 1929, Kate Roberts describes this phenomenon as it existed to Beti Gruffydd throughout her monotonous life, and creates there a strangeness little short of supernatural (though, I must stress, it was quite natural to Beti Gruffydd in her community). Here is the piece about her time-sense:

> If you'd have asked Beti Gruffydd on which Saturday during the summer she went to the seaside with the children, she wouldn't have been able to tell you exactly. But she would have been pretty certain she had taken them on the same Saturday in July through the years. The atmosphere of that Saturday could be felt before it came, and when it did come Beti Gruffydd and the children knew it was the Saturday to go to the seaside.

The other recurrence I want to note will lead to a short discussion of Kate Roberts's style of writing. Most communities admire eloquence. Eisteddfodau in Wales are popular because they are festivals organized to prove the cultivation of the basic human arts of singing, reciting and verse-making. Reciting was a particularly meritorious art in *Y Lôn Wen's* society, painful though it was always for the sensitive child performer (a late story, 'Dwy Gwningen Fechan' — *Two Little Rabbits*, treats of this). But in Kate Roberts's fiction it takes second place to the art of debate. Not organized debate, but the thrust of contentious speech, two characters trying to get the better of each other. More often than not the protagonists are women. Elin Gruffydd has a genius for the game, beating on the one side of the small social scale Mrs Huws the minister's wife, who is too prim even to think in public, and on the other Lisi Jên, who is too lazy. She has a quick brain, and a knowledge of loaded words, and a tone of voice that smites superbly. In *O Gors y Bryniau* the women are at it in three stories; of course in 'Henaint' the old woman gets the better of Wil with unnatural help.

As an example of this type of dialogue I'll quote a short piece from *Te yn y Grug*. Winni had eaten Begw's picnic, and afterwards chased Begw and Mair down the mountain before she herself was driven home by Robin, Begw's brother. He then escorts his sister home:

> When they arrived their mother was standing by the gate with Mrs Huws and Mair, an I-told-you-so look on Mrs Huws, a very worried look on her mother's face that turned into a welcoming smile.
>
> 'That Winni should be put under lock and key somewhere,' Mrs Huws said, 'she is much too old for her age, she's not fit to be among children.'
>
> 'Perhaps our own children wouldn't be any better had they been brought up like her, Mrs Huws. The girl never had a chance with a father like hers, her mother was a good woman.'
>
> 'H-m,' said Mrs Huws, 'they're ragamuffins, the lot of them. Like to like.'
>
> 'You, of all people, should know, Mrs Huws,' said Begw's mother, with her best emphasis, 'it was God's grace that led you to Trefriw wells and to meet Mr Huws and not Twm Ffinni Hadog.'
>
> She then took Begw's hand and pulled her through the gateway, and when Mrs Huws and Mair were turning towards their house she told Robin,
>
> 'You'd better thank Mrs Huws for the honour of saving Mair from the talons of Twm Ffinni Hadog's daughter.'
>
> And the doors of both houses closed.

Kate Roberts's outer and inner ears had been tuned to this kind of speech throughout her life. But critics commenting on her books — I among them — have all too often failed to recognize what it takes to form these dialogues. Yes, she had a fine ear. She also had a wealth of language. She elevated the colloquial words, phrases and idioms of her district, and used them as literature.

Many are listed in addenda to *Deian a Loli* and *Laura Jones*. The sharpest words are reserved for invective. There is a gem of a story in *Prynu Dol a Storïau Eraill (Buying a Doll and Other Stories*, 1969), where the chief character imagines his wife making a list of such words to denounce a former adversary. True, two or three of them were taken from the English, long ago, but what of that? — the fact that they cannot easily be rendered into English now shows that they circulate more freely in Kate Roberts's world; furthermore, it should be noted that borrowed words in time lose their exact original meanings and in the new tongue are given a slanted significance, are vivified by diminution or emphasis, or by tone of voice, and gain a new dimension when rhymed. Take this passage in Kate Roberts's Welsh:

> '*Dyma chdi yn poeni am fod rhyw silidón fel Williams wedi i ddewis yn flaenor a chdithau ddim: rhyw chwisl dun fel yna, sgellyn sgellog dau ben pennog, yr hislen ddefaid, y pendew stylcaidd iddo fo; yr hen standiffollach bach balch; rhyw chwidling fel yna, beth ydi o yn dy ymyl di?' Rhaid na ŵyr y bobl sy'n gweithio ar y Geiriadur Mawr ddim am eirfa Mari, neu mi fuasent wedi gofyn am ei help.*

The author is flying her colours, but she's got a reason for doing so! Here is an English version, with comments:

> 'There you are worrying about some minnow like Williams being chosen as a deacon and you not: a tin whistle like that, a small ribbed fin, two heads of herrin' [= herring, but I want to keep the rhyme —*in*: the phrase in Welsh has the lilt of mockery]; the sheep louse, the obtrusive thickhead; the weeny proud old waddler [the Welsh here has rhyme followed by alliteration — *standiffollach bach balch* — i.e. the elements of *cynghanedd sain*, a pattern of rhyme used in strict-metre poetry]; some shambler like that, what is he beside you?' The people who work on the Great Dictionary cannot know anything about Mari's vocabulary, or they'd have asked for her help.

The sense of seeing is also important in determining style. An author like Kate Roberts sees in nouns and adjectives, building with them an array of objects that embody and furnish her world. I have already noted how she clothes and feeds characters: clothes, food, furniture, animals, fields are described in detail that is never tedious because the descriptions are so precise and rich. The same eyes see comparisons and make metaphors, several of which (not unnaturally in this small world) recur time and again, the sinking metaphor about her own experience in 1921, the saying '"I wouldn't look at him through a quill"' (one of her mother's quips), and the group of metaphors that define painful vision as seeing thought or feeling the mind. Objectivity, rich description, the inclination for annalistic exactitude, these three qualities give her prose great clarity. Kate Roberts writes like an artist balancing on the borderline between imagining and recording, risking a fall sometimes, but seldom does she trip over to the scientific side. In truth, the few flaws of composition in *O Gors y Bryniau* are those of overconscious literariness, phrases and sentences which strain at binding the reader to the story, e.g. 'Now, if ordinary people like you or I would have been told this, we'd have fainted. But Ann Jôs was not an ordinary woman like you or I'. Such interpolations, popular at one time, only irritate us by their interference, and are not seen in later books.

VII

Kate Roberts's second volume of short stories appeared in 1929. It deals primarily with woman as wife and mother, with the attachments that create in her, repression, frustration, a feeling of romance, sometimes decay. A common contention in the stories of *Rhigolau Bywyd a Storïau Eraill* is that romance does not last. In 'Y Golled' (*The Loss*), the second story in the book, what is lost is romance itself. Indeed, it has been snuffed out of Annie's life before the story opens. The story describes her attempt to rekindle romance by taking her husband on an excursion to a favourite haunt of their courtship days. By now he had become 'Williams' and not 'Ted' to her as to everybody else. But near the lake this Sunday afternoon he seems quite happy, makes jokes, enjoys his tea, is Ted once more. Poor woman, she does not know that Ted agreed to come only because he wanted to skip Sunday School and avoid an argument there with a man called Lloyd. When Ted and Annie return home, one of his fellow teachers in Sunday School is waiting to give him news of how Lloyd that afternoon had been humiliated in the most remarkable way by one of the school's shy members:

> Annie did not hear the whole story, because she ran into the house to prepare supper. She was too happy to ask Jones to come and have supper with them.
>
> Her husband came in looking different somehow. As he ate he did not say a word, just stared at his plate of meat. She looked on the same thing, but her mind was far in the mountains. It retraced every act and every word and every glance of Ted's that afternoon. She was very happy. Ted was Ted after all.
>
> In a while, Williams said, 'I'd have given the whole world to have been at that Teachers Meeting this afternoon.'
>
> She nearly choked. Great tears collected in her eyes. But not for long. A moment later she laughed loudly and hysterically. Her husband raised his head and looked at her, amazed.

Had Annie been able to read the first story in *Rhigolau Bywyd a Storïau Eraill* she would have learned already that romance does not last. Had she been able to read the third she would have seen a girl evade its total loss by evading marriage itself. As in most working-class communities, in Kate Roberts's Arfon the economic necessities of life, more so than the social conditions, make of the marriage bond a bondage, a constraint that limits the wife to a narrow routine existence. Not for one moment does the author argue that a woman should break that bond and liberate herself — after all, where *is* the wide world for one like Beti Gruffydd who has never even seen the quarry where her husband has worked for thirty-two years? Anyway, his world is only made wider by the distance of the quarry from his home. Kate Roberts's literature is never a proselyte's: it is an observer's literature; she observes the effects of bad economies, rather than attacks what cause them.

For a woman such as Beti Gruffydd in 'Rhigolau Bywyd', existence is habitual not purposeful. She has no notions of melting hearts as Annie Williams has in more fashionable Colwyn Bay: but they do not breed de Beauvoirs there either. The irony of 'Rhigolau Bywyd' is contained in the fact that Beti becomes aware of the narrowness of her life and the pattern of her relationship with Dafydd her husband only when it is nearly at an end:

> Beti gazed at her husband for a long while. She had not reflected so much upon him since before her marriage. Then Dafydd was one in a thousand, but living with him had made him very similar to the rest of the thousand by now.

The next sentence in this paragraph connects the story with the second and with the third story in the volume. It reads:

> Beti had too much common sense to kid herself that the romance of love lasts very long after marriage.

It is an indictment of Annie and her effeminate faith; and it is the explanation of Geini's behaviour in 'Rhwng Dau Damaid o Gyfleth' (*Between Two Pieces of Toffee*). This beautifully constructed story is the *mabinogi* of Dafydd Tomos, now an old man cared for by his daughter and granddaughter, who gives him some toffee. Their making toffee reminds him of Geini who used to serve with him in Dôl yr Hedydd when they were young. Geini and he had fallen head over heels in love, but happy as she was in his company, time and again she postpones marriage, and once reiterates Beti Gruffydd's contention when she says '"once we marry, we'll become the same as everybody else"'. Dafydd's imploring makes her prepare a bottom drawer, but when the day comes for them to buy a ring, Geini flees from the watchmaker's shop. Dafydd has the grace to go away to work on another farm. Only once did he see her after that, one Saturday in town shortly after his marriage to Jane, when he saw her gazing into the watchmaker's window. Dafydd is brought back to the present when his granddaughter offers him another piece of toffee. The toffee-making shows us that he has not lacked the necessities nor the simple luxuries he could afford; and the history of his romance with Geini is contained by this frame of fact. His marriage, a soberer contract than marriage with Geini would have been, has outlasted romance in a way that cannot be measured. As for Geini, her return to the watchmaker's demonstrates that she was just as unsatisfied outside marriage as she knew she would have been within it. Marriage here then is sucked by a two-headed leech, longing and disappointment.

A more carnal longing, framed this time in fantasy, is described in 'Y Gwynt' (The Wind), the story of the passion an innkeeper's daughter feels for a sailor who fails to keep his promise to rescue her from her dreary surroundings. It is the wind that tells the tale, the wind being the reinspiration of the girl, who committed suicide; and it tells the tale to a lodger at the inn. This is the kind of story unexpected in Kate Roberts's canon. The only connections between her world and 'Y Gwynt' are the monotony of the girl's life and the sense of cosmic abandonment that pervades the whole piece. It is a bit fanciful, and reminds me (as it reminded Dr Pennar Davies) of a lyric by Kate Roberts's former teacher, John Morris-Jones. Kate Roberts's 'Y Gwynt' could be a prose exercise upon the last verse of Morris-Jones's 'Cwyn y Gwynt' (The Wind's Lament), where the insomniac romantic asks:

> Pam y deui, wynt, i wylo
> At fy ffenestr i?
> Dywed im, a gollaist tithau
> Un a'th garai di?

(Why do you come, wind, to weep / at my window? /
Tell me, have you also lost / one that loved you?)

Naturally, I do not deny a writer's right to surprise the reader. I welcome surprises — if only because they make the writer's 'authentic' world more vivid and natural. In the opening lines of the next story in *Rhigolau Bywyd a Storïau Eraill* we are back on Kate Roberts's terra firma. 'Meri Ifans married when she was twenty, and had a life common to many . . .' The sentence opens 'Y Chwiorydd' *(Sisters)*, another criticism of marriage which is a clean marble monument to sisterly love. *Rhigolau Bywyd a Storïau Eraill* was Kate Roberts's third book. *Laura Jones*, her fourth, came out in 1930. *Traed Mewn Cyffion* (1936) and *Ffair Gaeaf a Storïau Eraill (Winter Fair and Other Stories*, 1937), make the land of Arfon undisputedly hers.

This collection again contains quite a few stories about marital relationships, the most explicit of which is 'Y Condemniedig' *(The Condemned)*. Cancer confines Dafydd Parry to his bed and hearth. Thus — a device so often used by Kate Roberts — he has the opportunity to meditate upon the course of his life. His thoughts confirm Geini's fears in 'Rhwng Dau Damaid o Gyfleth' (they are our touchstone): he confesses that farm and household matters have taken most of his and his wife Laura's time; they have not been close lovers; and poverty, the end of a poor month, always made them uncommunicative. Now nearing death, Dafydd Parry wants to express that love so long unnurtured. He prepares mentally for the task. But when Laura comes to his bedroom what he recognizes in her eyes is not the flowering of love but a knowledge of his impending death. It is too late for love.

In all these stories about married couples Kate Roberts makes us aware of the effect the environment — nature, industry, the economy, — has on man's primary urge and the success or failure of the first human institution. Poverty deadens physical response, it also roughens the finer edges of marriage, leaving only habit. There is in all of them an undertone of disappointment. Man and woman are not fulfilled; life does not reach the beauty of its potential, because it is anchored in austerity. Only once does Kate Roberts directly criticize the government of the day for this impoverishment of humanity, in a story (situated in the south) about a protest march against the Means Test. There the husband is sceptical of the help the miners can expect from socialist politicians too. Amidst the public hope, his private cynicism is a reminder that greater powers than governments hold men down. For all this, though Kate Roberts describes most marriages as forces of habit, never does she allow one to break down in her first period of writing, partly because it is easier to face hardship in harness, and partly no doubt because such habits in Arfon are made of puritanical cement.

The soliloquy 'Meddyliau Siopwr' (*A Shopkeeper's Thoughts*) in *Rhigolau Bywyd a Storïau Eraill* is the first of three stories in that book and in *Ffair Gaeaf a Storïau Eraill* that pertain to a person very important in the 'life common to many' in Arfon. In the chapter on 'The Circumstances of the Period' in her piece of autobiography, Kate Roberts lists the local shopkeeper's mercy as one of two things that made life tolerable for the poorly-paid worker. Since the quarryman received his wages only once a month, his wife was often tempted to run a bill at the shop, a bill she sometimes could not meet; then she would be given credit.

> But after sharing out the money between the grocer, the butcher, the draper and the cobbler, there would not be much left to start another month. These things would often drag on until the heads of families finished rearing children. On the other hand it must be remembered that some families went deeper into debt than they should have done, insisting on having everything and taking advantage of the shopkeeper.

Kate Roberts has fictionalized both types of buyers, the ones who eventually clear their slates and the defaulters; and she looks at this aspect of life both from the shopkeeper's point of view and from the customer's.

In 'Meddyliau Siopwr' the shopkeeper is confined to his bed. There he imagines the scene in his shop that very moment, names and describes his favourite customers and damns his debtors, the chief of whom is Twm Defis whose four cows have disappeared overnight from the field opposite the shopkeeper's bedroom window. Try as he might to ponder over his other customers, his mind comes back all the time to Twm and the cows. When his wife comes home from the shop, she tells him that Twm's bailers had taken the cattle last night, and that there was no money for him.

But his fate is kinder than that of John and Ffebi Williams in 'Y

Cwilt' *(The Quilt)*, published in *Ffair Gaeaf a Storïau Eraill*. Over the years John Williams had extended considerable credit to his customers, who now, rather than pay their debts, prefer to pay for the goods big company-stores send up in vans. Consequently he is bankrupt, the victim of his society's disregard and his own kindheartedness. The story relates this history. But essentially it is the story of Ffebi's determination to fight in adversity: what symbolizes this is her resolution to keep a beautiful quilt she had bought when things were beginning to look bleak. In *Y Lôn Wen* Kate Roberts notes that R. Hughes Williams's characters abandoned the fight against poverty. Hers do not.

The third story involving a shopkeeper — this man is less sensitive than both the others — is 'Y Taliad Olaf' *(The Final Payment)*. He is made less sensitive because the author uses him as a symbol of life's unending struggle. Gruffydd and Ffanni Rolant this day have moved from the smallholding which had been their home for over fifty years to a private house. Their property and stock auctioned, Ffanni can now clear her bill at Emwnt's shop, a dream Jane Gruffydd in *Traed Mewn Cyffion* failed to fulfil. She loiters, dresses slowly, savouring this climactic moment to the full, and relives the several hundred Friday nights she had walked this way. 'This way from her house to Emwnt's shop was her biography.' Once or twice she could have cleared her bill, but her taste for fine linen and cloth had proved too great a temptation. Now it would be paid. But did that make her satisfied?

> Her turn came, and the shopkeeper did not say anything as she paid in full. He gave her a discount of half a sovereign, and that shocked Ffanni Rolant. She had expected half a crown. One thing that did not enter Ffanni Rolant's mind on her way down was the fact that she had paid over two thousand pounds to the shopkeeper since her marriage. She bought a few things and paid for them.
>
> 'More than likely I won't come down again,' she said. [Another shop, nearer her new house, had opened since she had started to have a slate at Emwnt's.]
>
> The shopkeeper nodded his understanding. She walked out of the shop. She groped for the latch, and latched it carefully after going outside.
>
> She looked through the grey window, and saw the shopkeeper poring over somebody else's book.

The vividness of this final look reveals all at once Ffanni's continuing attachment to this way of life — one payment does not change a lifetime's habit, it reveals her sympathy for the others who trek the same path, and it reveals in the shopkeeper's pose the continuance of the human struggle.

Side by side with this simple solid story, place 'Ffair Gaeaf' (*Winter Fair*), a diffuse tale about the activities of some mountain villagers who come to spend fair-day in town. I need not enlarge on that description of it here, except to say that the artistry with which Kate Roberts captures the disappointment of these people is so subtle, so brilliantly ordinary, it is as if the whole story was captured by a network of hidden cameras and microphones. I put 'Ffair Gaeaf' side by side with 'Y Taliad Olaf' because its diffuseness of description and characterization complements the conciseness of the other. Moreover, they say the same thing, emphasize the same life-routine.

In the three collections of short stories Kate Roberts published between 1925 and 1937 seldom do we feel that the stories have been written for our delight. Rather, they are a rendering of a world, affording us a knowledge of people and things in the light of a rare vision. 'Y Taliad Olaf' is only six pages long, but Ffanni Rolant is so familiar that we know she possesses all the qualities of Arfon's able women, all of whom can cook well, sew imaginatively, rear livestock, make butter, nurse the sick, manage meagre resources, prepare surprises. Dexterity and a capacity for courageous sufferance and wit make a triad of Amazonian characteristics. To these add good taste and refinement. And there in various degrees you have Ann Jôs, Ffanni Rolant as well as Jane and Elin Gruffydd, and Sara in 'Y Chwiorydd'. A description like this makes them appear most useful angels, and if truth be told Kate Roberts's eyeing of women is slightly askance (she loads evil unevenly — compare the good women with the two Sioneds in *Traed Mewn Cyffion* and with Beti in 'Y Chwiorydd'), but the women's basic intolerance makes them human enough. The men in these stories are mostly insensitive to mood and change, perhaps because work has made them tired.

It is easily seen that Kate Roberts knew her people. Because they were simple it was not possible for her to create a varied array of characters: simple folk are similar to each other; and to appreciate the subtle difference between them the reader must be a connoisseur of simplicity. Her treatment of them made her people sad, not always sad with sadness, but sad in the way the Welsh have adopted the adjective, *sad* meaning firm, discreet, quietly courageous — it is the sadness of a proud tribe in adversity. She once said of Thomas Hardy's poor men and women that they have minds 'where black is black and white is white, and the various hues that come between black and white [don't exist there]'. This is just as true of her Arfonians. They are unsophisticated. Nevertheless, again like Hardy's, they do experience happiness 'and they can say wise and intelligent things'. For the wisest among them in *Ffair Gaeaf a Storïau Eraill* the goodness of the world is already past. The Winter Fair is not what it was, and Ffanni's payment is made for a struggle already gone by. As she looks into Emwnt's shop on the way home, is that not a backward glance over life itself? Ironically enough, one important theme in Kate Roberts's books, even in the early ones, is the theme of the lost paradise of youth. I say it is ironic because so many of her chief characters constantly look forward to a better time.

VIII

The books containing Kate Roberts's early layer of life had been written before 1936. *Traed Mewn Cyffion* was finished before the summer of 1934, for it was awarded joint first prize in the novel competition in the National Eisteddfod held at Neath during that year. Five of the stories published in *Ffair Gaeaf a Storïau Eraill* had been printed in journals before the end of 1936 and perhaps even more had been prepared by then. Thus, the books published in 1936 and 1937 were the fruits of her labour in the period immediately before Kate Roberts's moving to Denbigh in 1935. After that date she was no longer the wife of a securely employed master printer who could steal a few hours here and there to write, but a partner in a business enterprise. During the next ten years much of her energy as well as her husband's was spent in consolidating their business, its printing-shop and the publishing house. This partly explains why the most important author of fiction to emerge in the 1920s, and one of the most prolific, failed to publish one book between 1937 and 1949. In a letter she once told me that perhaps it was laziness that kept her from writing. No, the years were busy: between 1937 and 1939 she helped to organize the Denbigh National Eisteddfod; during the same period she was in charge of a touring company of interlude players; and held an extra-mural class at Bylchau. 'But that's no reason for not publishing a book . . . More than likely I was not sufficiently agitated to write a book, and that's the true reason.'

Then of course war was declared. And naturally she was concerned at the suffering it created. Between 1946 and 1948 she organized among the readers of *Baner ac Amserau Cymru* what she called a 'Fund to save Europe', affiliated to the Council of British Societies for Relief Abroad. But the war did not directly affect her writing. Something that did affect it, especially her criticism, was the volcanic change in the psychology of Welsh nationalism caused by

43

the 'Fire in Llŷn', the burning in 1936 of the government's Air Training Centre in Penyberth, Caernarfonshire by Saunders Lewis, D. J. Williams and the Reverend Lewis Valentine. The Party had failed to stop the establishing of this Bombing School by constitutional means, and its leader had decided to act. To burn it was an act of honour and courage, of desperation as well; and it made people aware as never before of the forces from within and without that were destroying the native culture and civilization of Wales. The three incendiaries were personal friends of Kate and Morris Williams, and the Williamses were responsible for publishing the country's most influential Welsh weekly newspaper, which during the war carried Saunders Lewis's powerful commentaries *Cwrs y Byd (The Course of the World/World Affairs)*. How could she not be affected? But Kate Roberts had never been blind to these forces. Her early fiction deals much with the ending of a particular Welsh way of life, so does her criticism of the educational system condemn the Anglicizing of Welsh children. The 'Fire in Llŷn', the war, her own maturity, her position in Welsh literary circles, and her honest resolution, contributed to make her from about 1945 onwards a profound critic of life and literature in contemporary Europe. She desisted from introducing propaganda into her fiction — she would not make literature subordinate to something else — and became a newspaper columnist, made journalism literature, commenting in *Baner ac Amserau Cymru* and in *Y Ddraig Goch* on subjects that reflected the state of our civilization.

Her most stirring articles, and they are stirring partly because they are uncompromising, deal in the main with three subjects: the decline of spoken Welsh and the subsequent loss of the key to a great part of our cultural heritage; the state of contemporary prose, especially (but not exclusively) Welsh prose; she also has much to say on the morality that once framed the fabric of our life.

The first two topics are often treated simultaneously. An article published in 1949 on 'The Problems of Welsh Prose Writers' begins:

> It could be said that most of the problems of Welsh prose writers are rooted in the fact that we are not a free nation, and if Wales were independent I would venture to say that our problems would be quite different.

She notes four distinct problems. The first is an absence of tradition, or one might say tradition consciousness. Time and again she justly complains that scholars have given only scant attention to the study of Welsh prose, with the result that few modern writers have any knowledge of the classics. Secondly, because of our educational system and the great tides that have flooded our culture, we have lost the one thing that gives soul to all, the language's idiom. A good deal of the Welsh now written, she comments, is like well-translated English. Although their Welsh is generally poor — and this third point seems to contradict the second, but it does not — most writers are conscious of the decline of their language:

> and if a writer is a sincere Welsh writer, he cannot fail to be at one with his nation's past and at one with his nation's future also, and thus he strives to the best of his ability to keep his nation's literature and culture alive. Thus, he divides his life, interests and energy, and cannot give his whole life to literature.

He must fight for his language and at the same time create something with it. Her last point is a practical one again. Some say, she comments, that a Welsh writer has not got the time to create a novel. Kate Roberts says 'I used to believe that once, but I cannot say that I do any more'. In 1949 she believed that genius will out. What the Welsh lacked was not time, but young writers of vision.

Kate Roberts reiterated these complaints in several other critical essays and reviews during the next twenty years. She put one or two in paragraphs of fiction. In *Prynu Dol a Storïau Eraill* she describes an old woman talking to her dog

> in order to hear the old forgotten words of the Welsh language rolling over her lips, words like *ffaligragwd, gyrbibion ulw, straffaglio, newydd sbon danlli grai*. But the dog would not understand, no more than the young people of the present age.

These complaints constituted Kate Roberts's jeremiad. In her old age they made several young writers afraid of her judgement. One or two stood up to her onslaught and argued that it was easy for the likes of her who were reared in a monoglot society to choose correct Welsh words and master the Welsh idiom. In her answer, given in an address to the Honourable Society of Cymmrodorion who honoured her with a medal in 1961, Kate Roberts opened the windows on Europe and stated:

> The writers of other countries do not depend for their style upon the contemporary spoken language of their country. They study their country's literature; that is something most Welsh writers do not do, they read English, and it shows in their work.

Another writer challenged her statement that no one should write merely for patriotic reasons. Her answer again shows her appreciation of the practice of other writers in the world:

> it is not patriotism that should stimulate us to write . . . It is life that stimulates an author to write, life and all its problems, and people create those problems. When a man writes, he does not think of man as Englishman, but thinks of him as a human being, in relation to himself, or to his society, or to God.

The answer also plumbs the depth of her artistic conviction:

> It is not patriotism that stimulates us . . . but something much greater, a longing to express ourselves on matters that pertain to the whole of Creation, things dark to us, or things that pain us, or things that interest us that are neither dark nor painful. We cry out, we howl at Life, most often because we do not understand it.

A good portion of Kate Roberts's journalism was concerned with social values. She wrote extensively on the changes that had overcome Welsh life between her childhood and her old age, and wrote also on the effects of mass production and education upon the standard of our life and thought. These writings make manifest a spirit easily associated with the temper of her heroines — it is a Puritan spirit, a love of cleanliness, honesty and a belief in endurance; but a Puritan spirit with its vigour refined by good taste and sensitivity. In her columns on the traditionally feminine arts she kept alive a store of culinary terms and usages, and advocated two generations of Welshwomen to practise crafts that technology has tried to render obsolete. All this work, much of it done when lesser women would have been content to be celebrated, reveals a passion for civilization the women of Homer would have greatly appeciated.

His women of Lesbos would have enjoyed reading her columns on the power of the female in society. Both her imaginative and her actual world of Wales were in the main matriarchal societies; and in *Y Ddraig Goch* especially Kate Roberts was not loath to enlighten the modern wife on the subject of both parliamentary and marital politics.

IX

I have emphasized her critical and journalistic work. From 1946 until 1956 she undertook, over and above her literary work, to manage Gwasg Gee, for in January 1946 Morris Williams died suddenly. 'My world was shattered around me.' And as her brother's death in 1917 made Kate Roberts look upon the conditions of the society that reared her, so now her husband's death made her turn into herself, 'into my own thoughts' as she put it. But she did not write until her husband's death 'had cooled'.

The first literary fruit of her introspection was *Stryd y Glep (Gossip Row*, 1949), 'a book', according to one commentator, 'so different from anything Kate Roberts has written that we are urged to think the story belongs to a new author'. *Stryd y Glep* is 'a long short story in diary form'. The diary belongs to Ffebi Beca, a spinster in her late fifties confined to bed with paralysis of the spine. It covers a period of nearly five months during the third year of her confinement, months during which her life is changed by an external event. Her elder brother John decides to get married and leave home. This, Ffebi and her sister Besi fear, means a cut in their income; worse than that, it means accepting as sister-in-law a woman called Joanna Glanmor they just can't stand. The diary is a record of the progress of this 'event' and of Ffebi's adjustment to it. It also provides us with an examination of the characters who keep Ffebi company, and above all an examination of Ffebi's own character.

Stryd y Glep is a construction of part of the second layer of life in Kate Roberts's world, an inner stratum of problems and neuroses, where men and women are often intolerable and intolerant, but a world-layer where hope buoys humanity. The book ends with the quoting of a refrain from a *cywydd* by Siôn Cent:

Gobeithiaw a ddaw ydd wyf.

(My hope is in what is to come.)

This fifteenth-century poet is an apt and significant choice. Saunders Lewis once called him 'a poet of Christian pessimism'. Like all the classic critics of the here and now, Siôn Cent makes the world seem absurd by emphasizing its ephemerality, and condemns it because of the pain it causes him:

Rhyfedd ynof rhag gofid
Na'm lladd meddyliau i'm llid.
Ac eto, enwog ytwyf,
Gobeithiaw a ddaw ydd wyf.

(It is strange in me, faced with worry, / that thoughts that come to my anger do not kill me. / And yet, I am famous [? for it], / my hope is in what is to come.)

The transience of the world is clear to Ffebi also. In one entry in the diary she compares her friends and herself to 'small flies, judging each other as if we were gods'. During her illness the weekly meeting of these friends around her bed on Sunday nights had become a sort of private society — what Josiah Woodward called a Religious Society and Williams Pantycelyn 'Society Profiad' — that was for Ffebi a source of knowledge and comfort. But John's courtship of Joanna Glanmor, and a jealous housekeeper next door, wreck the society's privacy, and thus make Ffebi even more introspective, and nervous of the pain men and women cause each other. The diary now becomes her confessor — 'From one tribulation to another, until I'm nearly too weak to write. But I must write today to see if I can get rid of some of the pain that's on my mind.' She confesses to her own intolerance, and finally to her own self-centredness.

It seems perfectly natural that one should write of *Stryd y Glep* in religious terms, for Ffebi herself does so, explicitly. She sees: 'A crowd of thoughts following each other. Is there any escape from thoughts?' and says: 'Perhaps that is just another way of asking "Is there any hope of salvation?"' This entry ends with a metaphor the seventeenth-century author Morgan Llwyd would recognize: 'O! to be able to breathe and throw away this shell of flesh!' Another example occurs in the last entry but one, where Ffebi reaches what she calls 'the narrow pass of self,' a clear reference to a popular pulpit metaphor 'the pass of conviction' (was it originally Bunyan's?), through which the soul must go alone, on to the plains of faith and security. In the last entry, Ffebi gives a summary of her own spiritual condition and weaves a Siôn Cent-like synthesis of absurdity and hope.

The commentator who saw this book as something very different from Kate Roberts's previous works was correct in many respects. The setting is not Arfon or Glamorgan, it is a narrow street in a small town; the subject-matter for her is novel; the characters have a new inner dimension. No longer do we have *Traed Mewn Cyffion*'s chronological story about people placed on a piece of earth told simply. Far from being simple and straightforward — though the book is that too, compared say to the introspective stories written by J. Gwilym Jones earlier in the forties: this is not 'stream of consciousness' writing — *Stryd y Glep* is an allegory. The street itself is the world (just as Ellis Wynne's streets form his world in *Gweledigaetheu y Bardd Cwsc*); the parlour where Ffebi Beca lies is both salon and confessional, as everyone's house is sometimes. Does not Ffebi's illness represent man's imperfection, and the attitude of her friends and neighbours to it the faithfulness and fickleness of mankind? To keep a diary is to talk to oneself, a simple sign of man's basic madness; but to write well is to give that madness method, a shape, a civilized form. What Kate Roberts offers us as a layer of her new world is also a literary model of the actual world.

Yet some of the factors that constitute *Stryd y Glep* do belong to the old Kate Roberts. There is the emphasis on family ties, the mastery of language (especially of metaphor: this story is not glibly psychological, the reader can *see* Ffebi's psyche), and the attitude to life, so explicit in this book that it can be regarded as an acceptance of what had only been hinted at in the earlier fiction, most strongly in *Laura Jones*, whose heroine was much too young to define it satisfactorily.

X

It is significant that in the next two novels situated in her imaginative Denbigh, Kate Roberts retained many of the patterns (of behaviour and action) set in *Stryd y Glep*, and retained its theme. Ffebi's happiness at the end of the diary comes as 'a shaft of light . . . far from my past': her salvation comes from a 'previous happiness'. This is true again of Lora Ffennig in *Y Byw sy'n Cysgu* and of Bet Jones in *Tywyll Heno*, both of whom, like Ffebi, are pained by an unexpected problem that breaks upon the normal rhythm of their lives. Lora again keeps a diary; *Tywyll Heno* is told in the first person singular: thus the two later books are in part introspective and confessional. Most important of all is that Lora and Bet, like Ffebi, are placed in an emotional and psychological crisis from which there is no emergence except through self-examination. All three are 'suffering queens', as Professor Bobi Jones put it, able, self-regarding women who experience a loss that for a while destroys the equilibrium of their lives, an equilibrium regained only in isolation. One character who comes by now and again in *Stryd y Glep* and in *Y Byw sy'n Cysgu* to assist Ffebi and Lora is their minister Mr Jones. He is intelligent, true, but an understandable weakness for soft diplomacy is the chief characteristic of his personality. As if to emphasize this point, in the third novel, *Tywyll Heno*, the woman who suffers the loss is Mr Jones's wife.

Y Byw sy'n Cysgu is a relatively long novel, but it treats of only one event, or rather of the consequences of that one event, much in the same way as an ode by a poet of the princes in thirteenth-century Wales treated radially of one quality that characterized his patron: the novelist and the poet purposefully add to the central issue by wrapping around it layer upon layer of description, verification, proof, the several tissues of related emotions. The issue would lend itself to a simple lyric, or in Kate Roberts's case a short story, but no, it is amplified, so that the end-product is an edifice to a kind of artistic torture. The difference between the ode of the Gogynfardd and this novel is that whereas the medieval poet builds gothically, intricately, Kate Roberts builds simply, unassumingly.

Of all her books, *Y Byw sy'n Cysgu*, with its unrelenting ascertainment of grief, is perhaps the most demanding. The heroine does little to attract sympathy, though right from the beginning she is seen as the hard-done-by abandoned wife left to suffer the claustrophobic emptiness of her home and the suspicions of a hateful mother- and sister-in-law. Lora Ffennig is bold, some would say cold. Iolo Ffennig has run away with Mrs Amred. Why he went, is not known. But I would readily bet he absconded to get away from his wife's frigidity. The woman is able, handsome, house-proud, has all the gifts upon which Robertsian women pride themselves, but lacks tenderness; Lora is too righteous to be tender. As Kate Roberts will, she supplies that tenderness from Lora's sister's house, more especially from her sister's husband, Owen. The old Mrs Ffennig, Lora's mother-in-law, is Jane Gruffydd's mother-in-law reincarnated, and just as the old Sioned Gruffydd reared the wanton younger Sioned in *Traed Mewn Cyffion*, here in *Y Byw sy'n Cysgu* Mrs Ffennig and Esta (Iolo's sister) have influence over Derith, his daughter. The naughty girl is never her real mother's! In *Y Byw sy'n Cysgu* it is the old Mrs Ffennig who wears the 'masked horror of maternity' that contrasts with the harsh madonna of Lora, adored by her son Rhys.

Lest people turn against Lora, it is important to describe another aspect of her character portrayed in the novel. Seen from another viewpoint frigidity is cleanliness, and there is a clean honesty about Lora. Having lived a mundane married life, suddenly she's the independent woman, rid of the attachment. Difficult as it is to unravel freedom from frustration, that is what she tries to do in her diary. She has to use the diary because of the encroachments made on her privacy by her in-laws, her lodgers Loti and Annie, and by Aleth Meurig, a widower, who was Iolo's employer. These people sometimes add to Lora's frustration but again at other times make lonely freedom bearable. Within this framework it is logical that the one who adds most of all to her frustration, her grumpy old uncle Edward, is, in the end, the one who affords her the means to grasp her freedom. Lora goes to live in his house in the country with the children and Loti; and it is there that she records in the final entry of her diary how truly liberated she is:

> By digging and digging for [Iolo], and for my relationship with him, I feel that I have come to know myself better, by bracing myself I see that I have matured, and that there is in me a fountain that continues to rise, and give me an inducement to live.

This task, this psychological dig, the very exercise which has made her want to live has also, paradoxically, made her realize life does not make sense:

> Man has been a blockhead from the beginning, and because of his own faults he will be a blockhead for ever.

A necessary verification of this novel's grief is its criticism of the spirit of contemporary society. It is the late forties. Western Europe is beginning to experience the neuroses which the later Age of Affluence made into common ills. This dialogue between Lora and Owen is a criticism of the times and a link between the kind of suffering described in Kate Roberts's first period of writing and the new one:

> 'Isn't it strange, Owen? Take my father and mother having to leave this world comparatively young because of poverty. That was their pain. And we're not much better off with other pains.'
> 'There you go again, you still expect too much from some tomorow. I'll wager that your father and mother were quite happy bringing you up, [even] in poverty. They could enjoy the little things as they went along, and we've come to look forward to the luxuries.'
> 'Yes,' said Lora meditatively, 'There *are* some things worse than poverty.'
> 'Yes, their [kind of] poverty. What they did was fight against circumstances . . .'

Furthermore, the reader cannot help linking with these comments his fear of the fate of the children in Y Byw sy'n Cysgu, two sets, the Ffennigs and their country cousins, magnificently brought to life in the shadow of their father Owen's illness. Frank O'Connor has reminded us that creating in the novel 'a sense of continuing life is the thing'. In this particular novel it is the children, who go to school, need breakfasts, play or do not play, who wear out clothes and grow up, who supply that sense, because their needs — an omelette, a cardigan, a first dab of scent — force Lora and her sister out of their pains to do things, to practise womanhood. Come to think of it, *Stryd y Glep* is the only one of Kate Roberts's books that is childless.

Child-behaviour is a good barometer of the temper of the times, as Bet Jones, the minister's wife in *Tywyll Heno*, 1962, well knows. (*Tywyll Heno* means Dark Tonight. It is an epithet that alludes to one of the poems in a ninth-century saga about Heledd.) It is her son Geraint's loutish behaviour that first makes Bet Jones realize the incongruity between her beliefs and the world's behaviour. The novel is an account of the spiritual or psychological breakdown from which she has just recovered.

As she is a minister's wife, the novel is also a critique of the ethos of Welsh Nonconformity in the middle of the twentieth century. This aspect of the book spurred the Reverend Lewis Valentine to print a lengthy interview with the author in *Seren Gomer*, the Baptist quarterly. He asked Kate Roberts why she had undertaken to write about a woman of the manse. She answered by saying that she wanted to make 'the chapel the background for a story' — an inspired notion, for much of the weakness of contemporary Wales can be diagnosed as the loss of dynamic experienced over the last sixty years in our chapels, once the bulwarks of much strength: centres of worship, yes, and centres of Welsh culture as well. *Y Lôn Wen* contains a rich chapter on 'Culture and the Chapel'. There the author recalls the spirit of sacrifice in which her forefathers had built dissenting chapels in the quarrying districts, tells memorable tales about preachers and their sayings, and gives an account of the sort of education she and her contemporaries received in Sunday School and other meetings within their walls. Its worth, she concludes, was 'cultural . . . and not religious, unless the latter came indirectly'. When she was thirteen and fourteen years old (that is, in 1904-05), Wales experienced a scintillating attempt at a religious revival which excited large areas of the country; but Kate Roberts does not mention it in the autobiography. The revival is mentioned in *Traed Mewn Cyffion* — but only in passing: Owen and Twm were bored by the meetings, and when the time came for Owen to choose a career he was not attracted to the ministry, because 'there wasn't anything like that in the Ffridd Felen family'. However, chapel did provide a base upon which a young person could build his life, and it gave direction to that life;

that is, it provided a strict code of morals, a kind of security, and at the same time gave ambition a respectable lining. This it has continued to do until very recently even though its dynamic has diminished drastically. One of Bet Jones's comments upon her own situation when she began to feel she was losing her faith — for that is the loss experienced in *Tywyll Heno* — graphically describes the change between the two eras her life spans:

> I belonged to two worlds, the restrictive world of my youth, and the new world that I saw, heard and read about in books that did not recognize the wrong of sin.

Of course, Bet's loss of faith is not a particularly Welsh problem. Her experience is shared by a large section of Western society, it is what J. R. Jones termed *argyfwng gwacter ystyr* (lit., *a crisis of a void of meaning*), it is to be conscious of universal absurdity and to be pained by it. But Kate Roberts's decision to place this problem in a familiar Welsh setting gives it life. So do the characters of the book. Bet's husband, Gruff, like Mr Jones in the other novels, is a kind, intelligent man, but he is far too busy to attend properly to his family affairs, and he is the last person to realize what ails his wife. Their circle of good friends includes other ministers and good conventional chapel-goers called Mr and Mrs Bryn; it also includes Melinda, a young beautiful widow who tries to alleviate the loss of her husband by making the most of what the affluent sixties offer her. Mr and Mrs Bryn represent (though they don't *have* to be representative of anything, for they are dear, credible characters) — they represent what can still be admired in the spirit of Nonconformity, a sense of justice, coolness, ready sympathy: they administer what Gruff should administer. Melinda, on the other hand, is a small-town Jacqueline Kennedy Onassis: she does not allow herself time to brood, but flits hither and thither, to Paris, London, wherever, to escape what Bet *has* to face.

An important facet of *Tywyll Heno* is the variety of devices adopted by Kate Roberts as Bet to tell the story. We see the conventional stress on objects as symbols of feeling, and exactitude of description. The book contains a number of well-placed metaphors that illuminate problems, make them visible as it were. Take one example. In the opening part, Bet is still in hospital resting after treatment; she has been through her torment but as yet has not described it. Gruff is visiting her. She tells him,

'What if we knew what was going through everybody's mind here now?'

and he answers,

'God forbid, we could not stand it.'

Yet, as she remembers it, that is exactly the knowledge that first signalled her distress:

I could see much more than I saw before, as if the air was thinner, or as if there was glass instead of skin on everyone's head, and I was able to see through it to the base of their thoughts.

Later on, towards the end of the book when Bet goes berserk, Kate Roberts makes effective use of loose style:

. . . they try to talk cleverly in Society and Sunday School on what people should do and they themselves don't have an ounce of faith they don't understand the hymns and shout when they sing the tenderest things O blessed will be the shouts of the day to come I can see you Gruff are going to tell me I'm as bad as they are I know that I know that I know the others don't the world has destroyed itself . . .

This tirade is aimed at the lower middle-class matrons of Welsh or pseudo-English society. They are all aunts to *Traed Mewn Cyffion*'s Bertie Elis, Joanna in *Stryd y Glep* is their younger cousin, in real life they all hired colour television sets for Princess Margaret's wedding, and had convenient colds when the ex-prisoner Lewis Valentine came round to preach. They reappear in a few years' time in *Hyn o Fyd* (*What a World*); and in *Prynu Dol a Storïau Eraill* they make another, older reflection of Kate Roberts, very angry. According to Dame Helen Gardner, 'The writer's personal history, like the pressure of the age in which he lived, is a context which can help us focus on the work as it is', and that 'biographical knowledge can sharpen the sense of the work's objective existence.' The madams portrayed in *Tywyll Heno* were certainly part of Kate Roberts's personal world. They lived around her in Denbigh. Much of her journalism was a censure of their way of life — their Anglicizing of things Welsh, their abandoning real pride for peacock feathers: they (for Kate Roberts) were the mothers of our nation's ills, they turned our chapels into suburban clubs, and starved our culture of blood by giving birth to anaemic boy scouts. They knew nothing of Heledd, as Bet knows about her.

But for all their enmity, and notwithstanding her own loss of faith, Bet Jones in the end experiences a renewal of vitality, imagined once again as light. Heledd in the saga became demented after the loss of her brother. Bet recovers from her breakdown not as a result of divine intercession, but partly because she has examined thoroughly her attitude towards life. I say 'partly' because I cannot fully explain why Kate Roberts's later heroines are revitalized. Part of the answer lies in their own — and in the author's — nature. In the interview with Valentine she said that her greatest problem after Morris Williams's death was how to resist self-pity. Perhaps her characters have benefited from that resistance: in life and in literature Kate Roberts always admired the fighter.

XI

Her criticism of our age was published as a more general lamentation and in a less objective way in *Hyn o Fyd*, 1964. What I mean is that in the first two pieces (which constitute half the book) she abandoned conventional story-telling for reproach. 'Teulu Mari' (*Mari's family*) is a sort of animal farm, different from Orwell's in that the animals talk with Mari their mistress and don't live in a world of their own. Whereas Orwell's work is allegorical, Kate Roberts's story is not: it is a much less ambitious attempt to satirize this world's ways, it is really a device which gives the wise (and therefore eccentric) Mari an opportunity to utter plain truths. The second, brief piece in *Hyn o Fyd* is made up of three entries in a diary written after the great winter of 1963. It portrays the Kate Roberts I knew from her sadder letters, lonely, concerned, fed-up with the rottenness of things. She had come to believe that life as it was lived lacked purpose and that consequently people had become careless of everything except appearance. This was a recognition shared by many contemporary artists, and though she was surprised when a reviewer once coupled her with Samuel Beckett there is something to commend the match. Wil, in the last story in this book, could here be commenting on the playwright's work:

> We search for peace and contentment as if it were possible to have them; it's impossible to have them in a world so full of murder, thieving, dishonesty, prostitution, hypocrisy, niggardliness, . . . If we enjoy some part of our life, we enjoy it like seagulls skimming the surface of the water at the seaside, and forget, even in our profoundest moments, all the dirt and stink that's beneath us.

Taking my cue again from Helen Gardner, I should note that Kate Roberts's work is especially effective because it appeals to the reader's experience of the society in which it is set, and it forces him to identify himself with that society's ills. But that reader is an ideal reader. We must heed the Welsh! In our abnormality we are a nation nursing an inferiority complex so twisted that it is sentimentally regarded as a form of acquiescence. Actually it is a soft readiness to accept our own condition, and the world's condition, as if we could do nothing about the business. Those who read Welsh literature cannot ignore Kate Roberts's work. Yet there is a feeling among some readers — a feeling unexpressed in published criticism, but aired in extra-mural classes and in colleges — that her harshness is too cruel, that her view of life and the supernatural and human forces which control it is too disturbing. It is as if a people who have for so long abandoned the right to fulfil their own potential in things cultural and political do not want to know that what they have really abandoned is their share of responsibility in this cruel, degrading century. Even the 'happy endings' of the post-war novel and the long stories have not endeared her work to the majority, though of course they respect it highly and know its value. (And on a personal level she was much admired.) But the 'happy endings' belong to stories about a worsening world. In the first period her literature was about 'people who had backbone'; in the second period she reached 'an age when eels are trying to hold up the world', and her readers knew those eels well.

Kate Roberts made a general review of the state of civilization in many of the stories of her next three collections, in the second half of *Hyn o Fyd*, in *Prynu Dol a Storïau Eraill*, and in *Gobaith a Storïau Eraill*. Quite a few stories take the form of letters, or diaries, or a soliloquy, or again a miniature life-study. It is significant that when Kate Roberts wrote about her own maturing, the mark of change between childhood and adulthood was thought, it was thinking. The fifteen-year-old Kate noticed the change when she found she could not remember by heart a chapter she was to learn before confirmation. 'I am not happy,' ends the first chapter of *Y Lôn Wen*, 'I try to excuse myself, saying that I have a lot of learning to do at school. But perhaps by beginning to think about things, I cannot memorize as I used to.' The sensitive characters who figure in the stories I mentioned above are all blessed with this capacity for introspection and meditation. No doubt they are all Kate Roberts once removed. She made no attempt to disguise herself in at least one of the stories, *Dewis Bywyd (Choosing Life)* in *Prynu Dol a Storïau Eraill*, 1969, where the chief character is an author looking back upon the three great bereavements of her life, her brother's death in youth, her husband's in the prime of life, then another brother's a few years later. Kate Roberts refers to these deaths in an interview with Professor Caerwyn Williams, the opening paragraph of which is a rude abstract of 'Dewis Bywyd'. The author in the story finds that these deaths give order to her thoughts, indeed by now they are nursed and cherished experiences. The point is that for Kate Roberts the only person capable of judging life is he or she who has proved the very dregs of sadness. Judgement is made in Joseff's pit. Note that one of the characters in *Gobaith a Storïau Eraill (Hope and Other Stories)* states:

> It's worse on people who haven't reached rock-bottom, and haven't seen through everything.

Let us look at a few of these stories in criticism. Take firstly 'Yr Enaid Clwyfus' *(The Wounded Soul).* The story reveals in an excitingly easy style a panoramic view of the human condition, made from a mental hospital, where Jones, the Wounded Soul, is a patient. He meditates upon the sequence of events that led to his being taken there. Jones knows that the disappointment which immediately led to his illness was his being passed over in a chapel election for a vacant deaconship. But he also knows that this blighted hope is only one cell of the large cosmic tragedy of which he is conscious. This he feels all the more keenly because others around him — as represented by Williams, the schoolmaster who *was* elected deacon — are blind to the world's follies. Williams comes to see the Wounded Soul one day,

> and he said 'Don't worry, Jones, you'll be chosen next time.' 'There won't be a next time,' I said. 'O, you're not going to die,' he said. 'No, by hell,' I said, 'that's the most important truth you've ever uttered. Yes, the most important truth, I'll live again to be a thorn in your flesh.' 'You can never be a thorn in my flesh,' he said. 'No, for that matter, I can't, God gave you flesh that was too thick, and flesh too thin to me, but I can hear voices that you'll never hear.'

Those voices are Jones's salvation, they are his thoughts, his wisdom audible in his mind.

'Y Trysor' *(The Treasure)* in *Gobaith a Storïau Eraill* takes its place with other earlier stories in which a character looks back upon the years. Here the meditator is Jane Rhisiart. She has just buried her friend Martha Huws who only became her friend in old age, but Martha transformed her life. The opening sentence of the story reads:

> For the fourth time in her life Jane Rhisiart was trying to place the events of that life in their appropriate places.

We learn straight away that Jane Rhisiart is in full possession of all her faculties (the nervous and infirm review their lives four times a day not four times during their lifetime). We therefore await her orderly testament of the seasons. First of all she meditated in the late spring of life, when her husband left her. Then, in the Indian summer of her life, she thought about her children taking material advantage of her. The third time, autumn, was five years later, within a few months of her making friends with Martha Huws. And here she is again, Jane Rhisiart in the winter of her years, remembering the richness of her experiences with Martha, noting how they outweigh all the other things that had happened to her, so that now she could not tell anybody except Martha herself 'about the loss she had suffered through the departing of her friend'. For us that is ironic, as it would be for the Rhisiart children; but for a woman who had few treasures until she was sixty, that knowledge, that bond, even with a dead friend, is dynamic, life-giving. It is also an indictment of society's failure to share without stealing, to sympathize with a correct sensitivity.

In these stories Kate Roberts wrote more subjectively than of old, a trend noticeable in many authors who have aged with the ageing of this century's anguish. And things are spelled out; in literature all over Europe symbols have been made more obvious. Visits become excuses for conversation and confession, journeys are patently trips in search of paradise, questions asked in simulated innocence receive loaded answers, the simplest sentiment is a key to a primitive memory.

Consider 'Y Daith' (*The Journey*) from *Prynu Dol a Storïau Eraill*. It can be regarded as a full treatment of a scene composed once previously, in *Traed Mewn Cyffion*. There it was Wiliam who migrated to south Wales. In this story it is Dafydd who goes. But they are very alike. Some of the 1936 descriptions are repeated: it is a dark winter morning in both episodes, in the kitchen there is talk to fill the dreadful air of *hiraeth*, the father goes with the boy to the station, visits are made in an attempt to heal wounds. And of course Wiliam and Dafydd make the journey for the same reason. But 'Y Daith' is not an early story repeated by a flagging imagination. Rather the author chose to write it in order to emphasize poetically the meaning of certain things outlined in *Traed Mewn Cyffion*. In that novel, Wiliam's departure from Foel Arian was but one journey amid many, it was part of a larger pattern of diffusion. In *Prynu Dol a Storïau Eraill*, although we know the background well enough, Dafydd's journey is an isolated one, and therefore certain elements stand out clearly. I will note three. There is the trunk that holds Dafydd's belongings: his father and mother carry it and place it on the horse carriage 'as if they were carrying a sacrifice to an altar'; on the way to the station father and son sat with the trunk between them like a 'coffin'. Then on his way back up the mountain the father hears his friend Elin Wiliam say, '"I'd rather see a funeral going past than see someone on his way to the South"'. The image has been controlled masterfully. Of course, Dafydd is, so to speak, going to a new life, just as Dafydd Gruffydd in that day in the life of Beti Gruffydd in 'Rhigolau Bywyd' was entering a new stage of life. I mention Dafydd Gruffydd because the second important image in 'Y Daith' was first used in his wife's story. Though Dafydd goes to a new life in the south, what he takes with him as sustenance is the experience of childhood and youth, he takes what his mother gave him. In the train,

> When a fellow-traveller offered him a sandwich he had to refuse and open his own pack. The pressure-marks of his mother's fingers were on the sandwiches, and he nearly choked.

Lastly, the arrival. The novelist did not take us right into south Wales with Wiliam. He was left in the train plucking up courage to face the coal-mine, a confident enough ending to a tragic chapter. In the story Kate Roberts completes the journey with Dafydd even unto his lodgings where there was a clean table laden with food, 'and the bright light of the gas lamp . . . falling on the whiteness', a sure and, by now in her work, familiar symbol of hope.

An exceptionally fine story, both symbolic and 'objective', and one that has 'metaphysical resonances' *pace* Simone de Beauvoir, is 'Cathod Mewn Ocsiwn' (*Cats at an Auction*), published in *Hyn o Fyd*.

What Elen observes at the auction is, seemingly, the betrayal of an old friend by a group of women. What they really betray is Life itself. Not only are they catty, as the title suggests, they are vulture-like as well, pecking away at a life which they had once made tolerable. They destroy their own creation, they are moral cannibals. The women have come straight from the pages of *Tywyll Heno*, and within earshot of Elen (who had come to the auction to bid for a cupboard) they criticize the dead Mrs Hughes for being poor and for keeping a shoddy house. Elen is pained at this, and in her sympathy for Mrs Hughes sees the ruffled carpet on the floor taking the forms of her nose, ears, mouth, forehead:

> Elen stared long at the face expecting to see the forms change, and see one expression of a smile for her because she had given [Mrs Hughes] one kind thought. But she did not get one.

The next second someone tramples on the carpet,

> [trampling] the face of the dead in her coffin.

When she gets home Elen decides to ask her solicitor to change a part of her will: she wants all her furniture to be stored together in one place until it rots.

XII

Kate Roberts published two other collections of stories, *Yr Wylan Deg* (*The Fair Gull*) in 1976, and, finally, a few months before her ninety-first birthday, *Haul a Drycin a Storïau Eraill* (*Sun and Storm and Other Stories*) in 1981. The latter is a very short collection. It contains one story about Winni Ffinni Hadog that was first published in *Y Faner* in 1963; it contains also another two stories about Winni written especially to accompany that older one. The three portray Winni now growing up in service, holding back her swear-words, going to chapel, blackleading grates, Winni facing the embarrassments of menstruation, and Winni gradually (but only gradually) getting away from the harassment of being Twm Ifan's daughter. The author here could not resist returning to her favourite. I now have little doubt but that her favourite is — or, rather, in her original fury, *was* — a fictionalized construction of part of Kate Roberts's own repressed self. It was not merely Mrs Huws the minister's prudery and snobbishness, and not merely the Denbigh ladies' anti-Welsh attitude that made Kate Roberts fulminate against them; she knew that their pinched morality, their narrowness of outlook, their cosy conservatism, their conventional chapel-going, was, like it or not (and Kate Roberts often did not), part and parcel of the established Nonconformity which couched her own religion and which housed so much of the culture she wished in wisdom to preserve. There was in Winni, for a time, a girl who could rail against all that as Kate wished to rail, and kick against the traces of dutifulness, respectability, and the dullness that often accompanies these things. Like the final story in *Te yn y Grug*, the Winni stories in *Haul a Drycin a Storïau Eraill* are stories of chastening.

The other three stories in this collection, strangely enough (for I doubt whether it was planned in that way), span the time zones of Kate Roberts's whole literature. One describes a very young couple starting out in life, and is set in the Arfon of the mid nineteenth century when many of the quarries were merely mined outcrops of slate and when the great Victorian preacher, John Jones Tal-y-sarn (d.1857), was the Methodist leader in those parts. Another describes the mental breakdown over a century later of a working-class wife whose eventual recovery-signs allow her unemployed husband and son to celebrate her improvement with tongue for supper. The third story takes us again into that personal hinterland where the chief character is but a slightly veiled portrayal of the elderly Kate Roberts herself. If this were a biographical study I could easily verify (from my own knowledge of her and from the testimony of others) that nearly all the experiences described in 'Gwacter' (*Emptiness*) happened to her: long periods of treatment in hospitals, her relationships with nurses and doctors, her determination to construct new stories, her complicated domestic arrangements, even her coidentification with the young Jane of her imagination who marries the minister. *Haul a Drycin a Storïau Eraill*, her final book, though one of her poorest, is nevertheless a significant contribution to her literature, for it is in part a subconsciously patterned summary of all that went before, it is in part also a sort of forced farewell.

An editor would not include in her *Selected Stories* any story from that volume, whereas he would certainly include at least two or three from *Yr Wylan Deg* and would have to consider a few others. Here, Kate Roberts's powers are still formidable. (Ailments and age made creative thinking and writing difficult for her from about 1978 onwards.) *Yr Wylan Deg* contains two stories that were first written a quarter of a century previously. Both of them depict old women, one in Arfon, one in Denbigh, facing death and concerning themselves with the dispensing of furniture and life-savings. I have an inkling that Kate Roberts aged quickly after Morris Williams's death — that is, that she aged in attitude. Having remained uncollected until 1976, these stories now take their place with several others concerning old age and with stories that contain the uncompromising life-commentary of old age. Indeed, even some of the youngsters portrayed here, Sam and Wil in 'Dau Grwydryn' (*Two Tramps*) and 'Yn ôl Eto' (*Back Again*), and Mair in 'Torri Amod' (*Breach of Promise*), look at life with the resigned ironic acceptance one sometimes associates with age. Sam and Wil had taken a sabbatical from schoolteaching to be tramps, but realize at the end of that year that they can not escape:

'At least we've had a go and in my opinion even if we took to the road [again] before long we'd realize that we'd meet difficult people there as well. You can't be rid of people.'

Mair is just twenty-one, newly engaged to be married. But a visit to an old aunt that gives her a glimpse of 'a great monotony, the monotony of affliction, the monotony of nursing the sick, the monotony of life' prompts her to regard her marriage not with anticipation but with the question 'What then?' So she breaks her engagement. It is not unfair to ask whether by now Kate Roberts had imbued many of her characters with her own outlook on life, and made them cyphers.

She had become, in Saunders Lewis's indelicate but true description, 'an old woman living alone in Denbigh', pained by leg-ulcers and loneliness, bored by her condition, world-weary. She had always been disgruntled and critical, more often than not perhaps disgruntled and justly critical. Now, that disgruntledness became much of the stuff of her stories. It is not difficult to portray her in her confinement — at home or in a hospital ward — as one eyeing our small corner of civilization like a mindful ancient commenting on things rather than story-making about things, although, again, as between what I called the 'scientific' and the 'fictional' in her earlier works, the borderline between commenting and story-making in her case is pretty thin. 'Cwsmeriaid' (*Customers*) in *Yr Wylan Deg* is an opportunity for another Robertsian shopkeeper nearing retirement to review the lives of a catalogue of customers and customer-types. Of course, as one would expect from a pen as pointed as hers, the shopkeeper's observations are both entertaining and telling, as lively and life-giving as good literature should be. But the story is still a commentary.

These two books are, of course, valuable in themselves, but they are valuable also because they confirm some things about Kate Roberts, the solid and awesome simplicity of her imagination, the plainness of so many of her sayings and comments (but, as I suggested above, before long it will be necessary to reassess that simplicity and plainness: beneath them there lies, perhaps, an underworld of repression). In this essay I have stressed the change in attitude and in setting that characterizes her two periods of writing. It is obvious that the two hemispheres of her world are complementary and have much in common. One early imaginative pattern I commented upon after

discussing *O Gors y Bryniau* and *Rhigolau Bywyd a Storïau Eraill* was
the dialogue kept up by two women who behaved as if they were
playing out a ritual of reasoning. In *Gobaith a Storïau Eraill* and in *Yr
Wylan Deg*, there are several groups of friends and of sisters who live
together whose behaviour towards each other is an interesting
contrast to that of the early debaters. In the Denbigh half of her
world, in the broken society of our day, Kate Roberts places new
importance upon close companionship, upon the spiritual helpmate;
the mountain society of old Arfon regarded itself as an organic unit in
which such warm formalities were unnecessary. Tension makes
people bubble over with talk, confess not debate. Stylistically, this
means that the later volumes contain the dialogue of meditation;
axioms and epigrams appear more often. Ffebi Beca, for instance,
says that: 'Romance is not seeing the other side of things.' Another
character sees the days of the future as hundreds of mice that came
out of their holes to the dark. She is Marged Parri in 'Te P'nawn'
(Afternoon Tea) who strings together so many witticisms that she
raises the spirits of her melancholic minister. Such pains do not
bother the Arfonians of her Victorian and Edwardian ages; or else it
can be put in another way: they could not afford to mope. But they
were bothered by a supernatural oppression, a kind of fate. Can it not
be argued that the spiritual cancer that now knaws away at ministers'
souls and at the psyche of unfortunate women is but a new image of
the old mystery that envelops mankind? Kate Roberts is brave
enough — and has been followed in this by one or two younger Welsh
writers — brave enough to investigate the disease of the age, though
it means that to many she is 'displeasing as a writer'. Now, Time holds
no terror. Indeed, all would like to turn the clock back. But when
people wished for a better time, Time went at such a rate that Kate
Roberts recorded their disappointment at 'going through life without
living it', a magnificently aweful phrase. Where is happiness? It is only
in hope. In both periods the author has created intelligent sensitive
people who have recognized mankind's struggle against these forces,
and who have fought against defeatism.

Yet I feel there is one important change. The early stories in, say,
Rhigolau Bywyd a Storïau Eraill seem to have the power of tales written
after years of oral transmission. The later stories are more intense,
and in them the author is more intent upon making smooth the pleats
of pain. Perhaps the change can be symbolized in the difference

between Kate Roberts's view of Beti Gruffydd and her view of Lora Ffennig. What happens to Beti Gruffydd is that a thought strikes her, gives her pain, becomes a problem as big as life itself. She meditates about it all day carrying her past around with her in her head, but is all the time engrossed in her chores as well. Kate Roberts stands aside and records. Lora Ffennig loses something, is pained, yes, but the pain now is something that changes her life, and when she meditates about it she does so on paper, working out her own salvation — with the author's help. What I mean is that Kate Roberts gives the impression of one going under Lora's skin, becoming Lora, willing her regeneration. The difference is the difference between Arfon and Capel Mawr Dinbych, between the Mabinogi and Methodism.

Kate Roberts died in 1985. She had lived for ninety-four years, and for sixty years and more had written about people of all ages in two distinct periods and two distinct settings. It was as if she had been around in the land of Lleu, Gwydion and Arianrhod since the first half of the nineteenth century when the elder Sioned Gruffydd of *Traed Mewn Cyffion* first came as a girl from Llŷn to do service in Arfon; she experienced the Great War, saw Welshness ebb; went to Denbigh and damned its pretence, its surface culture, its hypocrisy; but, remaining there, became a source of knowledge and sympathy, in story after story taking her sad or sick Denbigh people back to her mountain home, back from what she saw as the pity (and, sometimes, the absurdity) of the human situation, back to Mother Earth, before discharging them fitter and finer to face again whatever future there will be.

A Bibliographical Note

It will be useful for non-Welsh readers to know that some of Kate Roberts's work is available in English translation. Wyn Griffith translated *Te yn y Grug* as *Tea in the Heather*, 1968, and Idwal Walters and John Idris Jones translated *Traed Mewn Cyffion* as *Feet in Chains*, 1977. Twelve of her early stories, 'Two Storms', 'The Wind', 'The Loss', 'The Quilt', 'Old Age', 'A Summer Day', 'Between Two Pieces of Toffee', 'The Letter', 'Final Payment', 'Sisters', 'The Condemned' and 'Folded Hands' were collected as *A Summer Day and Other Stories*, and published in 1946. 'The Loss' also appears in Alun Richards (ed.), *The Penguin Book of Welsh Stories*, 1976. Wyn Griffith's translation of 'Cats at an Auction' was published in Gwyn Jones and Islwyn Ffowc Elis (eds.), *Twenty-Five Welsh Short Stories*, 1971. And in 1981, in celebration of Kate Roberts's ninetieth birthday, Gwasg Gregynog published *Two Old Men and Other Stories*, the other stories being 'The Treasure', 'Visiting', 'Buying a Doll', 'Old Age' and 'Winter Fair'.